NEW APPROACHES IN SOCIOLOGY
STUDIES IN SOCIAL INEQUALITY, SOCIAL CHANGE, AND SOCIAL JUSTICE

Edited by
Nancy A. Naples
University of Connecticut

A ROUTLEDGE SERIES

New Approaches in Sociology
Studies in Social Inequality, Social Change, and Social Justice

Nancy A. Naples, *General Editor*

"BETWEEN WORLDS"
Deaf Women, Work, and
Intersections of Gender and Ability

Cheryl G. Najarian

Routledge
New York & London

Published in 2006 by
Routledge
Taylor & Francis Group
270 Madison Avenue
New York, NY 10016

Published in Great Britain by
Routledge
Taylor & Francis Group
2 Park Square
Milton Park, Abingdon
Oxon, OX14 4RN

Transferred to Digital Printing 2009

International Standard Book Number-10: 0-415-97912-9 (Hardcover)
International Standard Book Number-13: 978-0-415-97912-2 (Hardcover)
Library of Congress Card Number 2005034071

Library of Congress Cataloging-in-Publication Data

Najarian, Cheryl G.
  "Between worlds" : deaf women, work, and intersections of gender and ability / Cheryl G. Najarian.--1st ed.
        p. cm. -- (New approaches in sociology)
    ISBN 0-415-97912-9
    1. Deaf women--United States. 2. Deaf women--Employment--United States. 3. Work and family--United States. 4. Deaf women--education--United States. I. Title. II. Series.

HV2545.N35 2006
331.4087'20973--dc22   2005034071

ISBN10: 0-415-97912-9 (hbk)
ISBN10: 0-415-80572-4 (pbk)

ISBN13: 978-0-415-97912-2 (hbk)
ISBN13: 978-0-415-80572-8 (pbk)

informa
Taylor & Francis Group
is the Academic Division of Informa plc.

Visit the Taylor & Francis Web site at
http://www.taylorandfrancis.com

and the Routledge Web site at
http://www.routledge-ny.com

For Mom, Dad, and Mark

Contents

List of Tables

Acknowledgments

I dedicate this book to my mother, Patricia Najarian, my father, Aram Najarian, and my brother, Mark Najarian. Without the love and support of my family, this project would not have been possible. Thank you for giving me the confidence to begin and the courage to finish.

I also dedicate this research to the women of this study and their families who generously gave their time, energy, and input. I thank them for their willingness to share their lives. I am forever shaped by their stories.

I thank Marjorie DeVault who has served as an invaluable mentor to me. I feel honored to have her as a colleague and friend. I would also like to thank other readers of my research who include: Susan Borker, Madonna Harrington Meyer, Julia Loughlin, and Steven Taylor for all of their time and energy which helped me to shape, question, and articulate my ideas. Thank you also to Nancy Naples, Series Editor, for her thoughtful comments and to Benjamin Holtzman and the staff at Routledge for their efforts as my book took its final form.

I wish to thank the many friends and extended family members who were also an invaluable system of support. Friends who have especially supported me during this project include Amy Tobin, Laura McBride Wadsworth, and Michael Schwartz. I thank them all for their encouragement and faith in me. Finally, I wish to thank my friends and colleagues in the Sociology Department, the Women's Studies Program, The Center on Human Policy, and The TA Program and The Graduate School at Syracuse University and the Sociology Department and the Center for Women and Work at the University of Massachusetts Lowell.

Chapter One
Introduction

In an ever changing workforce, the experiences of women both at home and in the paid work sector have undergone radical changes in recent years. These changes have influenced the shape of families and workplaces that we have come to know today. The experiences of people with disabilities in the workplace, particularly those of women who are seen as "disabled," have also undergone dramatic shifts. One such group to consider is deaf women, who are seen by some as "disabled," but who also argue that they are bilingual and part of a linguistic minority. What can deaf women, in their positions as mothers and workers, contribute to our ideas about work and family? As these deaf women navigate their ways in these various work and family settings, we gain interesting insights into our ideas about women, work, disability, and family life.

This study, then, will address the invisible and visible work that deaf women do in their family, educational, and work lives to negotiate their identities. A major theme in this research is how the women describe experiences of being "between worlds" in these aspects of their lives and how they carve out places for themselves in the Deaf world, hearing world, and the places in between. Through semi-structured, open ended interviews, this research investigates this work and shows how it is done in a larger social context, which has rendered it as seemingly innate and invisible. Through feminist methodologies and qualitative research, this study puts women's everyday experiences and paid and unpaid work lives at the center of sociological analysis with the intention of understanding how their work is organized, performed, upheld by larger social institutions, such as the family, schools, and workplaces, and serves to create and maintain women's identities. This project also uncovers the implications this work has for women, families, and children.

REVIEW OF RELATED RESEARCH

My study draws on and contributes to several bodies of literature. I will first address the literature which focuses on education and deafness. In addition to these schools of thought, I will also include a discussion of unpaid work and deafness as well as a literature review of paid work and balancing mothering and paid work. As part of this overview, I will also make brief mention of the connections between bilingual women of color and the deaf women of this study.

Education and Deafness

Overview of the Deaf Community

Members of the Deaf community consider themselves part of a linguistic minority who have a shared native language, American Sign Language (ASL), history and culture which is separate from the hearing world (Padden & Humphries, 1988). The Deaf community differs from those who identify as deaf, where the latter usually refers to those who are defined by the medical definition of "the audiological condition of the not hearing" (Padden & Humphries, 1988). People who are deaf are often, although not always, older Americans who lose their hearing and become deaf later in life and do not consider ASL their native language. There are also those who consider themselves hard of hearing, which is seen by the Deaf community as a more acceptable way to name what the medical discourse defines as "hearing impaired." Instead of viewing themselves as people who have an impairment or something that needs to be fixed, hard of hearing people use this term as a political way of identifying themselves and resisting medical notions of deafness. Many hard of hearing individuals, although not all who define themselves in this way, consider themselves as part of the Deaf community.

According to recent research, there are, in the United States, approximately twenty to twenty-two million people that are hard of hearing and one and a half million who are deaf (Bruyere, 2004). According to scholars at the Gallaudet Research Institute (GRI), the National Center for Health Statistics (NCHS) also provides similar national statistics, which are gathered from the National Health Interview Survey (NHIS); however, as the GRI rightly points out, this and other reports do not provide estimates to indicate those who were born deaf or hard of hearing and those who lost their hearing later in life (Holt, et., al., 1994; Mitchell, 2002). Also, it does not include estimates of those who consider themselves part of the Deaf community. Therefore, we simply do not know how many Deaf, deaf, and hard of hearing people there are, much less those who are college educated women.

Although these statistics create a murky picture, we do know that the Deaf community is a strong one which has various regional and state Deaf Clubs, foundations, and its own private non-profit organization, The National Association of the Deaf (NAD). Founded in 1880, NAD is the oldest and largest organization which safeguards the accessibility and civil rights of deaf and hard of hearing Americans in education, employment, health care, and telecommunications (NAD website, 2002). Their website includes position statements of the organization on various salient issues for the Deaf community including education opportunities, employment options, cochlear implants, and information about Deaf culture.

One of the most important issues for members of the Deaf community has been to be recognized as a linguistic minority rather than as people who have a disability and whose deafness needs to be fixed. This can be seen in the NAD's view on the Deaf community's official stance on cochlear implants, a device that can be surgically placed in a deaf person's cochlea to presumably "improve" their hearing. The procedure is costly and involves wearing an apparatus that attaches to the outside of one's ear and also inside to the cochlea and connects to the waist. It also requires that individuals go through speech therapy and often be part of a support group after the operation so that they might adjust to their new identity. In some cases, individuals who have a cochlear implant operation experience a "decrease" in their hearing "abilities," while for others they notice that they are able to hear sounds more clearly. According to the NAD's website (2000), the Deaf community's official stance on cochlear implants is that: "Cochlear implantation is a technology that represents a tool to be used in some forms of communication, and not a cure for deafness."

While wanting to remain open to the technology of cochlear implants, the NAD argues that the Deaf community and hearing world should not view deafness as a disability and something that needs to be "cured." Others who have a more radical view of the use of cochlear implants argue that it is one way in which the medical community "colonizes" the Deaf by encouraging them to be more like hearing people and discouraging the Deaf to use their native language of ASL (Lane, 1999). While the controversy regarding cochlear implants continues to be debated in the Deaf community, it is also connected to another area of discussion on deaf education.

History of Deaf Education in America

According to Baynton (1996), there are two major historical events that served to organize deaf education and the history of the deaf in America.

The first was the founding of the first school for the deaf, the American Asylum for the Deaf at Hartford, Connecticut, in 1817 by Thomas H. Gallaudet and Laurent Clerc. In 1815, after studying in Paris with the French teacher of the deaf, the Abbe Sicard and his student, Laurent Clerc, Gallaudet, who had traveled to Europe to learn about deaf education, was impressed with Sicard's method of teaching the deaf through sign language. He asked Clerc to accompany him back to America where they established the first deaf school with Clerc as the head teacher. This first of many residential schools was located near the sizable deaf community on Martha's Vineyard, where many deaf individuals had begun to develop their distinctive community, culture, and language (Groce, 1985). The second major event in America regarding the history of the deaf and deaf education was the formation of a group of reformers, in the late nineteenth century and continuing on into the twentieth, led by Alexander Graham Bell and others who favored eugenics and who sought to undo this growing deaf community. They favored prohibiting "manualism," or the use of sign language, both in and out of the classroom and replacing it with "oralism," which relied on teaching the deaf to communicate using only lip-reading and spoken English.

As Baynton (1996) argues, these two ways of organizing deaf education were actually reform movements, which were embedded within particular moments in American history. Manualists were evangelical Protestants who viewed the use of sign language as a way of converting people who might not, in their minds, have previous access to the gospel. Oralists, in the late nineteenth-century, were instead concerned with the "national community" and thought more in terms of "scientific naturalism" and evolutionary theory than about religion (Baynton, 1996, p. 9). Oralists associated those who used sign language with inferiority by equating them with animals and used deaf schools as a place to eliminate sign language and "normalize" the deaf.

Throughout the twentieth century, deaf children in America were segregated into both oral and manual residential schools for the deaf and were not allowed equal access to hearing schools. With the Disability Rights Movement of the 1960s and passage of the Individuals with Disabilities Education Act (IDEA) of 1975, grew the concept of "mainstreaming" where deaf children were put into public hearing elementary and secondary classrooms. Unfortunately though, deaf children and their parents had to fight for the right to have sign language interpreters in these schools as a "reasonable accommodation" for their deafness and the Supreme Court denied them that right (Smith, 1996). Many of the women of this study experienced their early years of elementary and secondary education at this time and were often mainstreamed without the assistance of sign language interpreters or note takers. The effects of this denial on the Deaf community in America have often been equated with a type of cultural genocide and termed as part of the "failure of deaf education" (Foster, 2001; Lane, 1999). Experiencing this kind of education, many of these women and others in the Deaf community have described the feeling of being "between worlds." Due, in part, to the set up of our school systems, they have struggled to find places for themselves in the Deaf world, hearing world, and the places in between.

With the passing of the Americans with Disabilities Act (ADA) in 1990, deaf children and their parents were able to advocate more effectively for the right to sign language interpreters and support in public hearing elementary and secondary schools. As Baynton (1996) outlines, the new term for mainstreaming has become "inclusion," which proposes to integrate deaf students into local public schools. As he describes, the debate of deaf education today is mainly between mainstreaming, usually with interpreters who use a manually coded English system such as Sign Exact English (SEE) or cued speech rather than ASL, on one side, and those who support a bilingual and bicultural education that uses ASL as well as English (Baynton, 1996). Oral schools (schools where ASL is forbidden) still exist in the U.S. today and now many of them go under the guise of "cochlear implant schools," where the students have had cochlear implant surgery. These different educational experiences have made it challenging for the Deaf to communicate among themselves, since various deaf individuals still, to this day, may not learn ASL until they reach college. In fact, some may never learn ASL at all or "pick it up" somewhat from interacting in the Deaf community. The TTY (telephone for the deaf) and electronic mail have aided in the Deaf community's ability to gain access to each other, but barriers in terms of learning a similar language still remain due to the structural organization of deaf education programs and schools.

Educational opportunities for the deaf and hard of hearing have been somewhat broadened by the ADA, however, there exist only three colleges in the U.S. that have sizeable programs which are geared toward Deaf people: Gallaudet University, the National Technical Institute for the Deaf (NTID) (a college within Rochester Institute of Technology), and California State University, Northridge (CSUN). Gallaudet University is the only Deaf university in America and where the March 1988 protest, Deaf President Now (DPN), occurred. During this protest, two thousand deaf students, faculty, and staff rose, rejected their newly appointed hearing president who they forced to resign, and elected their first ever new deaf/Deaf president Irving King Jordan (Brueggemann, 1999). This moment was a major turning point in Deaf education and speaks to the strong Deaf community that exists at Gallaudet University. Similar and yet also different from this community, are the campuses of NTID and CSUN. The Deaf communities on these campuses are part of the larger hearing culture of their universities and are thus more a mix of Deaf, deaf, and hard of hearing individuals. For the women of this study, these postsecondary options and limited choices were important influences on how the women developed their own identities as Deaf women and saw themselves as part of the Deaf community, hearing world, and the places in between.

Despite the increase of educational opportunities for deaf women to attend college, many may find themselves searching for a job where they feel both challenged and socially integrated. Often, social integration becomes a barrier and causes many deaf women either to go work in the "deaf world" or to become stay-at-home mothers. Thus, it appears that many deaf and hard of hearing women are working in jobs that their college education seemingly over qualifies them for and that track them into working with the deaf: working as teacher's aides in deaf education programs in both predominantly hearing and deaf schools, as teachers and administrators in schools for the deaf, at deaf camps, or at deaf daycares. Certainly this is not true for all college educated deaf women; however, a large majority of them seem to experience this. My research uncovers how these college educated deaf women, who are seemingly privileged by their education, experience their paid and unpaid work lives. It also investigates the structural challenges that they encounter and how they resist these challenges in their daily activities.

What is (Dis)ability?

Recently, the field of disability studies has undergone major changes in how scholars as well as activists define the term "disability." This scholarship has also had an influence on as well as been influenced by the field of Deaf studies. What follows is a brief overview of some of the major literatures in these two fields as well as how it relates to sociology and this project on deaf women and their family, education, and work life experiences.

Erving Goffman's (1963) sociological conceptualizations of stigma as a kind of "spoiled identity" or deviant status have been used by various disability studies scholars to discuss how people who are seen as disabled have often been marginalized in society. Higgins (1980), who did a sociological study of the deaf, used Goffman's framework along with Becker's (1963) concept of "outsiders" to argue that the deaf were outsiders in a hearing world. Much of the scholarship at this time was focused on the idea that people with disabilities, such as the deaf, were seen as the "other" rather than fitting the "norm" in society.

Other sociologists have been interested in viewing "disability" through a different lens from the perspective of deviance and instead called for a "sociology of acceptance" (Bogdan & Taylor, 1987). Further, they argued that "handicapism," much like notions of racism and sexism, was linked to theories of representation in our culture (Bogdan & Taylor, 1977). This research prompted sociologists and disability studies scholars to think more critically of how we have come to know what we know about definitions of the term "disability."

Drawing on and included in this literature, various scholars further emphasized that disability is a social construction, that it is another sector of oppression, and that it is linked to issues of representation in various discourses such as the medical, education, and legal discourses (Bogdan, 1988; Bogdan & Biklen, 1977; Bogdan & Taylor, 1994; Linton, 1998). Linton (1998) also argued for a "claiming" of the term disability and argued that we need to put disability studies at the "center" of our analyses because it adds, as she states: "a critical dimension to thinking about issues such as autonomy, competence, wholeness, independence/dependence, health, physical appearance, aesthetics community, and notions of progress and perfection–issues that pervade every aspect of the civic and pedagogic culture" (p. 118). These perspectives greatly inform this study of deaf women and their experiences in their family, educational, and work lives. This project seeks to put deaf women at the center of analysis and to call the term "disability" into question.

Another contribution to the fields of sociology and disability studies has been the notion of performing or passing for "normal" in various contexts (Goffman, 1959). The idea that deafness is an "invisible" ability or disability in certain contexts is informed by these perspectives. This is also an area where scholars often collide with disability rights activists and those who are proud of their "disabled" identity. Scholars who consider the Deaf community as a legitimate and visible linguistic minority as well as notions of Deaf Pride and history are important aspects of this literature and what the Deaf community sees as the claiming of their identity as a civil rights issue (Padden & Humphries, 1988; Shapiro, 1994).

Some scholars argue that a constructionist view risks missing important connections between disability, bodily pain, suffering, and materiality. For example, feminist disability studies scholars have focused on the body as a site of analysis to show how ideas of ability, disability, and gender become embodied as well as how they relate to cultural notions of "able bodied" workers (Thomson, 1997; Wendell, 1996). These literatures inform this project on deaf women by pushing us to think how theories of disability relate to the concept of being part of a linguistic minority and connect with the body as a site for sociological analysis, particularly with regards to technology in the work place.

Deaf Studies: What is Deafness?

Various scholars have theorized what deafness actually means. For example, as stated earlier, some argue that the Deaf have their own culture because of their language, ASL, experiences, and history and advocate for putting Deaf people at the center of our analyses (Padden & Humphries, 1988). Others show us that we cannot think about deafness without also thinking about race (Herring Wright, 1999). Higgins (1980), as mentioned earlier, uses the theory of outsider/insider to write about how the deaf can often be seen as outsiders in a larger hearing world. He links the deaf with other groups that are often seen as outsiders, such as people of different races and sexualities, to show how there are similarities among these groups and how the term outsider is largely a result of time and space. Other authors who either write about what it is like to be deaf themselves, to be a parent of a deaf child, or to have deaf parents complicate the notion of outsider/insider and loosely touch on issues of unpaid work with regards to women in families (Davis, 1999; Herring Wright, 1999; Smith, 1996; Spradley & Spradley, 1978).

There have also been theorists who have argued that deafness is a social construction (Baynton, 1997; Lane, 1997) and one where identity is based on an interpretive process of interactions between and among people across various times and spaces. Within the theory that the deaf are socially and culturally constructed, various authors also argue that the deaf are a linguistic minority (Bauman & Drake, 1997; Lane, 1999). Unlike an essentialist position where one might focus on individual differences, these authors also recognize that the Deaf are a linguistic minority in a larger hearing society context. Lane, in particular, uses colonial theory to show how the deaf are a linguistic and cultural minority who are at risk from losing their freedom. Likewise, Davis (1997) argues that the redefinition of the deaf as a linguistic minority in Europe in the eighteenth and nineteenth centuries, much like races, nationalities, ethnic groups, and nations was a political venture which was linked to the growth of nationalism. Still other scholars have considered how the construction of deafness is contingent on time and space (Baynton, 1996; Groce, 1985).

Foster (2001) argues that there are three models for looking at disability, which include the medical, social construction, and political models. In terms of similarities between deafness and disability, she argues that they both share a history with the medical model, that both deal with issues of culture and colonization, and that in both fields there is a controversy about the role of non-disabled or hearing people in research. In terms of the differences between disability and deafness, Foster states that some argue that the deaf, as I have mentioned, are a linguistic minority. She points out that some argue that the integration of the Deaf into schools is a type of "cultural genocide" (p. 111). Foster also argues that while disability advocacy focuses more on the connection between cultural consciousness and political action, deaf people are more apt to join together to form social networks (this is not to say that the Deaf do not join at *all* for political reasons). She also mentions how most culturally Deaf people, unlike some people with disabilities (although not all), want to be named as Deaf. Her argument, then, is that deafness is both similar and different to the category of disability and because of this we should take a "multi-dimensional perspective" when looking at the deaf (p. 117).

These literatures guide my research in terms of how to think about the term "deafness," especially with regards to women and unpaid work. My work investigates how various constructions of deafness play a role in the paid and unpaid work of these deaf women. It also looks at how identities vary *among* deaf women. It is my position that deafness, or more accurately the stigma that we attach to it, is a social construction; however, I also recognize the embodied aspects of deafness, and the idea that the Deaf may be a minority group in a larger hearing society and that this status can and has changed over time and space. The aim of this project is to show how this occurs in these women's family, school, and work settings.

Unpaid Work and Deafness

Unpaid Work, Invisible Work, and the Role of the Family

Like other scholars, I view the family as an institution which plays a critical role in establishing and maintaining women as those expected to do particular kinds of work (DeVault, 1991; Harrington Meyer, et. al., 2000). I also, as others do, view the family as a social construct where the positions of mothers and fathers are gendered on the basis of certain ideologies that we have of masculinity and femininity (Coltrane, 2000; Gubrium & Holstein, 1990; Lupton & Barclay, 1997). These ideological constructs and the social structures that exist to uphold them, lead us to believe that the roles of mother and father are natural ones; however sociological perspectives allow us to question if they are indeed "natural" positions. This research will look at how this applies specifically to deaf women in their paid and unpaid work lives; however, I also seek to show how these deaf women navigate their identities and how this relates to the experiences of other women who also do the work of mothering.

The literature on mothering and families is essential to my study of deaf women because it provides a language for talking about this work as gendered. It also helps make this work visible as well as to uncover how it is constructed, embedded, and reinforced in the daily lives and activities of these deaf women. Following the work of Smith (1987), I seek to show how beginning with the everyday experiences of these women's daily lives, we can uncover and make visible their work experiences, which contributes to our sociological knowledge of women, the family, and mothering. The term "invisible work" has often been used by feminist sociologists to describe unpaid work such as mothering, which may or may not be visible in various contexts (Daniels, 1987; DeVault, 1991). Others have written about "emotion work" which uncovers efforts made in terms of family feeling (DeVault, 1999; Hochschild, 1983). I seek to broaden our sociological ideas of "invisible work" and "emotion work" by including a discussion of how the deaf women of this study communicated in their personal relationships, with their husbands, with their children, and in their role as activists.

DeVault (1991) shows how the work of feeding a family, care, and sociability is often relegated to mothers; she also shows how it varies by race and social class. Other authors, who focus on the family and work, show how some women are doing double and sometimes triple duty with regards to mothering and paid work (Hays, 1996; Hochschild, 1989, 1997). Additionally, various authors have shown how these experiences vary by race and social class. For example, while middle class women often have a choice about whether or not to work as mothers and also for pay, many working class and women of color have been doing double and sometimes triple duty even before the feminist movement and the women's employment revolution (Amott & Matthaei, 1996; Collins, 2000; Glenn, 1987; Hochschild, 1989, 1997). The paid and unpaid work that these women do is interrelated and dependent on each other and also serves to uphold the division of separate spheres that has existed in our culture.

My research builds on these ideas of the sociology of mothering as a kind of invisible work and adds to it the experiences of deaf women who do the work of mothering. This study investigates the experiences that these deaf women have in their families and how they negotiate their own identities with those of their children. This research shows the work that they do when making decisions about how to educate their hearing and deaf children, both formally and informally, and how their decisions are received in both the hearing and deaf worlds. This project echoes and builds off of scholars who connect the unpaid and often invisible work of mothering that is done between mothers and school teachers (Griffith,

1995; Griffith & Smith, 1987; Harris, 2003). For the deaf women of this study, language and whether or not to teach their children ASL, SEE, or to use oral methods, also becomes a key factor in the invisible work of these deaf women in their positions as mothers and how they identify themselves. By incorporating this into my analysis, my study highlights how language becomes a key part of this work, not just for the women of this study, but for all mothers, especially those who consider themselves part of a larger linguistic minority.

Another area of unpaid work which my project uncovers is the deaf women's role as activists. Traustadottir (1992) has written about the extended caring role of mothers who have children with disabilities and how this is a kind of activist work. Naples (1998) has shown how mothers of minority groups view their mothering as a kind of activism. The deaf women of this study do a similar kind of activist work by making various decisions about their own languages and those of their children. They make political decisions about teaching their children ASL and being part of the Deaf community or teaching them spoken English so as to resonate more closely with the hearing world. Also, many of the deaf women of this study are highly involved members of the Deaf community in organizations for the Deaf, research projects on women with disabilities, and in Deaf organizations for women. This study uncovers this unpaid work in the context of mothering and how they make decisions about involving their children in these kinds of activities.

How does Disability Fit with Unpaid Work?

Scholars have studied disability and unpaid work in a variety of ways. Some have argued that women with disabilities have struggled, in certain contexts, to be seen as viable and visible mothers (Reinelt & Fried, 1998), while others have drawn a link between the idea of disabled women as nurturers and aesthetics or "attractiveness" (Asch & Fine, 1997). Still others have looked at disability with regards to families to see how they sometimes subvert the stigma of a label of their disability (Taylor, 2000) or how sometimes in families where children have disabilities parents play "stereotypical" roles of mother and father in an effort to "normalize" the family (Traustadottir, 1992). No sociological study has been done on college educated deaf women and their families with regards to their unpaid work and how it might relate to or differ from the above claims. These perspectives guide my research on deaf mothers because they provide a way of thinking about the influences that family and mothering have in both their public and private lives and the work that they do in their lives.

Paid Work

Navigating Spaces

Scholars such as Ahmed (2000) and Lugones (1990) discuss how as bilingual women of color they experience a kind of border crossing in their lives where they seek feeling at home. Although some of the experiences of these women involve more literal border crossings than the deaf women of this study, there are interesting connections between these experiences. The ways in which these deaf women experience their work and family lives in terms of finding a sense of place or community will also be explored. This project will show how these deaf women were often tracked into working in the deaf world, especially in schools and colleges for the deaf.

Paid work is often studied by feminist scholars to explain the separation of spheres between men in the paid workplace and women in the home as a result of the Industrial Revolution (Reskin & Padavic, 2002). Other scholars look at how this sexual division of labor resulted in occupational segregation, which tracked various women into certain occupations and professions where they are paid less and have less power than men (Jacobs, 1995; Reskin & Roos 1990; Stone, 1995). Scholars have also investigated how paid work might be not only gendered, but also how experiences differ among women of various races and social classes (Amott & Matthaei, 1996). Other studies have looked at issues of channeling and choosing and argue that women who are considered part of a racial minority are often tracked into certain professions (DeVault, 1999; Sokoloff, 1992).

Few scholars, however, have included women with different abilities in their analyses and there exists no study of college educated deaf women's experience in the paid workforce. Barnartt (1997) did investigate gender differences in both educational and occupational attainment for deaf individuals over time; however, while her work is a significant contribution, it does not address the connections between the paid and unpaid work experiences of deaf women. This research, then, looks at the paid work of deaf women while connecting it to their unpaid work lives. As these women negotiate places for themselves in their working environments, they also do the work of developing their identities as women. This study uncovers the various obstacles that they face in these environments and how they struggle to resist these barriers in efforts to become part of the deaf and hearing worlds. Language becomes a key factor in how they find places for themselves in their working environments and in how they are able to resist being stigmatized for their deafness.

Problems with Thinking of Paid and Unpaid Work in Binary Terms

The authors in the book, *Working Families,* (2001) edited by Hertz and Marshall (see Galinsky, 2001; Gerson & Jacobs, 2001; Moen & Han, 2001), among many others, contend that the paid and unpaid work that women do are inextricably linked. Along with this group of feminists, my research looks at both paid and unpaid labor and the everyday practices of these deaf women in an effort to highlight this link. These scholars work to unpack the myth of a binary public and private divide between work and family. While adding to these literatures, my research will look at the similarities and differences of these connections for deaf women. My research investigates the paid and unpaid work of deaf mothers to better understand how their identities form and change in the deaf world, hearing world, and the spaces in between.

How does Disability Fit with Paid Work?

Various scholars have looked at women with disabilities and paid work and argued that these women face a double discrimination; one on the basis of their sex and the other on the basis of the perceived disability (Blackwell-Stratton, et. al., 1988). Others have made the claim that women with disabilities have not been part of the women's employment revolution of the 1970s and 1980s and instead of struggling to be "supermoms" have fought for the right to be workers and mothers (Russo & Jansen, 1988; Thomson, 1997). As mentioned earlier, little research has been done on college educated deaf women and work. Thus, my study will be grounded by the above mentioned literatures, but will also uncover the experiences in the workforce for this particular group of women. It will also help us to better understand the role of education and family experiences in their daily lives and career paths.

How does Deafness Fit with Balancing Paid and Unpaid Work?

Unfortunately, there is a dearth of sociological literature in this area of study. To date, there are no national data on deaf individuals and work. Gallaudet University has done some research which looks at the elementary and postsecondary education of deaf individuals, but does not focus on how this education may influence work decisions and family dynamics. Some research has been done by researchers at the National Technical Institute for the Deaf (NTID), who have looked at deaf schools and work. Little research has been done, however, on what happens to deaf people who go to college or looked at this topic in terms of gender, race, and class. Researchers at NTID are doing some of this now as a small piece of a larger study and their preliminary data shows that deaf men and women feel socially isolated in their jobs, which leads many deaf women to become stay-at-home mothers (S. Foster & J. MacLeod-Gallinger, personal communication, March 21, 2002).

AN OVERVIEW OF THE STUDY

This research addresses the seemingly invisible and visible work of college educated deaf women in their paid and unpaid work experiences. Specifically, it looks at how they negotiate their identities in their family, educational, and work environments. As mentioned earlier, a major theme of this research is how the women describe the experience of being "between worlds." The women describe sometimes feeling a part of the Deaf community or "deaf world" while also feeling, at times, part of the larger hearing society or "hearing world." Their experiences of being "between worlds" take many forms. The women also describe simultaneously feeling a part of both "worlds" and, depending on their family, school, and work contexts as well as their decisions to use ASL, spoken English, or a combination of communication methods, work to develop their identities in these aspects of their lives. The women also use the term "between worlds" to describe the differences *within* these two worlds and how they identify themselves and later make decisions about how to communicate with their husbands, children, and colleagues. "Between worlds" is a thread that runs through all of the chapters and as the meanings of it shift, so too do the women's sense of themselves.

This study begins with the methods and procedures, which make up Chapter Two. Chapter Three uncovers their family and educational experiences and the decisions they and their families make about their educations. Chapter Four looks at their work as mothers and activists. In this chapter, the women show us how they make decisions about their own identities as well as the influences of these decisions on their childrearing. It also explores the role of activism as a kind of unpaid work, which aids these women in developing their identities. Chapter Five looks at their paid work experiences, how they balance their mothering, paid work, and activism, and how they are often in between the worlds of the deaf and the hearing. Lastly, Chapter Six offers some concluding remarks as well as suggestions for future research and our ideas about how identities are created and negotiated in the daily unpaid and paid work lives of women.

Chapter Two
Methodology

This study investigates the everyday lives of college educated deaf women in their educational, family, mothering, and paid work experiences. It is grounded in the everyday work experiences of college educated deaf women in two different geographical locations or communities. Following scholars such as Smith (1987) and DeVault (1991) who begin with the everyday experiences of women's lives while also putting them in a larger social context, I seek to show the links between the work lives of these women and such institutions as the family, schools, and workplaces. The idea of unpaid work as labor, which as various scholars have shown is often gendered and relegated to women, is another perspective I use in framing this study (DeVault, 1991; Lorber, 1994). Since scholars such as Hertz and Marshall (2001) illustrate that paid and unpaid work are inextricably linked, I sought to investigate the women's both paid and unpaid work lives to gain a richer understanding of their experiences. Using this as a framework and putting these women's experiences at the center of my analysis, I looked for places in these women's lives where they did the seemingly invisible, sometimes visible, and unpaid work of mothering, educating people about their deafness, and self-advocacy.

Since the work of these college educated deaf women, who might be seen by some as "disabled," has never been written about, I wanted to make these women's experiences visible to people who may not be familiar with this group and also, as others have done, to question our ideas about "disability" (Linton, 1998). As I investigated the women's lives, which often included being stigmatized because of their identities, I also sought to uncover the places where they resisted various obstacles put before them in their educational, family, and work experiences. In this way, I follow scholars who argue that we can achieve a more complete understanding of oppression when we uncover the process of how it works and the spaces where individuals resist being oppressed (Sandoval, 2000). I used qualitative methods, specifically life history interviewing, as a way of getting at the women's experiences in their paid and unpaid work lives in an effort to understand how this all worked or the processes by which they experienced their daily lives.

QUALITATIVE METHODOLOGY

In these life histories and through the process of qualitative research, which uses interpretive, descriptive, and inductive approaches, I investigated the work lives of these college educated deaf women. Qualitative research grows out of the *Chicago School* tradition which includes interpretive approaches to our social world as well as the belief that our knowledge of realities is socially constructed (Berger & Luckmann, 1966; Bogdan & Biklen, 1998; Glaser & Strauss, 1967; Taylor & Bogdan, 1998). Following this tradition, I also took the approach that this way of doing research is descriptive or a way to get at people's everyday experiences and observable behavior (Bogdan & Biklen, 1998; Taylor & Bogdan, 1998). Qualitative research is also an inductive type of investigation where researchers seek to ground theory in the data or experiences of people's everyday lives (Emerson, 2001; Glaser & Strauss, 1967) as well as being open and flexible to changing as additional data is collected (Bogdan & Biklen, 1998; Emerson, 2001; Taylor & Bogdan, 1998).

Interview and Life History Research

While conducting in depth interviews with these deaf women, I used a combination of interviewing practices, which included semi-structured and open-ended interviews (Bogdan & Biklen, 1998). Using Holstein and Gubrium's (1995) method on the active interview, I began my interviews as one would begin a conversation, which also had a "guided purpose or plan" (p. 76). This method allowed me to have some order to the interviews so that I could ask similar questions of each respondent, while also leaving a space where the women had the opportunity to discuss their lives in their own way. I did this, as others who use feminist interviewing methods have done, in an effort to resist imposing how I would organize their lives onto the ways in which they wanted to tell their stories (Reinharz, 1992).

Also in line with feminist methodologies and interviewing methods, I worked to make visible the life history experiences of these women as a group which has not previously been written about so that we might gain a fuller understanding of the multiplicity of women's experiences (DeVault,

1995). Following scholars such as DeVault (1999), DeAndrade (2000), and Best (2003), who look at how race and ethnicity are socially constructed within interview settings, I tried to continually think about this process, as they suggest, even if it did not appear on the surface of everyday talk. This study then also investigates the role of language, such as American Sign Language (ASL) and spoken English, the politics of "talking" in particular ways, and the effect that this has on our understandings of these deaf women. Like Reinharz (1992), who suggests that situating oneself is another tenet of feminist methodologies, I continued to think about my role in the research process and its effect on this study of college educated deaf women.

Situating Myself in the Research Process: Social Locations and being "Between Worlds"

During our interviews, there were various instances where the women taught me about the Deaf community or ASL. Through our communications, we were constantly negotiating being between the Deaf and hearing worlds. This occurred as we slipped in and out of ASL, Sign Exact English (SEE), English, and used lip reading, body gestures and sometimes even writing and pictures to tell the stories of their lives. Although I am the one who writes up our conversations and an interpretation of their educational, family, and work experiences, this research also suggests that *how* we communicated to collaboratively construct these life histories influenced these stories, as in any study.

My social location of being a hearing woman with a Deaf brother and knowing SEE and some ASL has shaped my own experience of often feeling in between worlds. This social location, as with any, has influenced my interactions with these women as we constructed the stories of their everyday lives. An interview with Teresa illustrates how this affects our constructions of hearing, deafness, and the places in between:

C: Because it's harder now to communicate with my brother.

T: (She nods and mouths, "oh really?")

C: Because he is now ASL fluent and I'm like "what?!" (laughs)

T: (She gives the sign for "right" and smiles.)

C: He also knows Sign Exact English, but I notice when I talk, similar to you, he watches my face.

T: Well, ASL people look at the face because they see the emotion in the face. They sign. If you were here (She rolls her index fingers down and looks down at the table like she is signing to the table and so I cannot see her face.), they'd be missing the face. They cannot see if you are really serious or if you're joking or so it (She gives the sign for "important.") The only time they look at the hands is when they're finger spelling. Some of them (She makes a motion with her hands and says "poooh.") and I have to look down. (I think she was meaning that they sign fast.) It varies with people, because I'm not native, so I still have to ask people to go slow.

As we negotiated how we would communicate in the beginning of this interview, I describe to Teresa how, as my brother has become more fluent in ASL, this has affected how we communicate in our family. Although I am not fluent in ASL, the way that I structure my sentence by saying that he is "ASL fluent" instead of saying that "he is fluent in ASL" is arguably ASL and not English grammar. Despite me not knowing ASL, I, in some ways, go back and forth in our conversation between the languages of ASL and English. At the same time, I was also signing in SEE to Teresa, which suggests that although I am not bilingual, I am doing the work of negotiating between worlds in order to communicate with her.

Although Teresa might not consider ASL her native language and describes people who are native ASL speakers as "they," which seems to suggest people other than herself, there are moments when she uses ASL in our interview. My brother explained to me that when Teresa says "poooh" and makes a motion with her hands, that she was speaking in ASL to describe people speaking fast. Teresa also goes back and forth between the languages throughout our interview by signing and talking in English and then by completely dropping her voice as she does when she signs, but does not verbally say, "important." These examples suggest that she, like myself, was negotiating being in between worlds in an effort to communicate with me. It also suggests that through my somewhat "insider" status of having a Deaf brother, I was able to see this moment in a particular way.

These types of nuances occurred in every woman's interview. As the women discussed their experiences of being in between worlds in their family, educational, and work lives, they, as well as I, were doing the work of going back and forth between these worlds. While doing this, we worked together to negotiate what it meant to be deaf, hearing, or somewhere in between and developed strategies, such as modifying our languages, in order to communicate and tell the story of their lives.

DATA COLLECTION

I began my study of college educated deaf women with the following research questions:

- How do deaf women with a college education experience their paid and unpaid work lives?
- What barriers do they encounter despite the privilege of their education and what strategies do they use to resist these barriers?
- How do barriers and places of resistance vary for college educated deaf women (in paid and unpaid work) for those who are actively employed in a Deaf community versus those who may be isolated from a Deaf community?

This topic grew out of my previous research where I did a life history of a college educated Deaf woman and her family (Najarian, 2002). Various themes which emerged from this study fueled my interest for exploring how college educated deaf women experienced their paid and unpaid work lives. I became increasingly interested in the similarities and differences between those women who had oral educations and those who attended manual schools and colleges for the deaf and the influences this had on the women's lives and career opportunities. This woman from my previous research, as well as other personal and professional contacts in the Deaf community and those who work at NTID, served as invaluable consultants for me as I continued on with my research.

Through these contacts, who I met with on an ongoing basis beginning in February 2002, I was able to get in touch via email with ten college educated deaf women who had worked for pay and were also mothers. The first phase of data collection, where I conducted ten in depth life history interviews in either the women's homes or offices so that I might observe them in their paid or unpaid work environments, took place beginning in June 2002 and ended in March 2003. The women chose where they would prefer to have the interviews as well as a time that would be convenient for them. Eight interviews were in women's homes and two were in their office environments. The interviews lasted from one and a half to three and a half hours, the average being two and a half hours. Although I gave all of the women the option of having a sign language interpreter present for whom I would pay, only one requested an interpreter. All of the interviews, with the exception of Stephanie's interview, which was not audio taped, were video and audio taped and later transcribed. Each woman, with the exception of Beth who had a sign language interpreter and Ellen, whose husband was also present for the interview, was interviewed alone.

As I gathered more data, I also worked, as Glaser and Strauss (1967) suggest, at simultaneously analyzing the data while I was gathering it. I coded by hand throughout the study and refined my questions based on emerging themes from the data collection. After I finished phase one of my data collection, I began phase two, which consisted of contacting the women for follow-up interviews. I did this in an effort to get a fuller picture of their lives as well as to take the opportunity to share with them some of the major themes of the study. Phase two of my data collection took place from May 2003 until July 2003. Follow up interviews were conducted via email and nine out of the ten women responded. As with the first interviews, these interviews were semi structured, open ended, and active, as I wanted to see if there was anything else that the women wanted to add to their life histories.

Respondents

I interviewed five college educated deaf women who lived in Rochester, New York and five women who lived in Boston, Massachusetts.[1] Rochester, located in upstate New York, is the home of the National Technical Institute for the Deaf (NTID), a college within the Rochester Institute of Technology (RIT). Since NTID is a college for the Deaf, deaf, and hard of hearing and housed within the larger hearing college of RIT, it is unique in that, unlike Gallaudet University in Washington, D.C., which considers itself an all Deaf college, NTID attracts students, professionals, and staff who come from a variety of perspectives, but for the most part are interested in being in a place where Deaf, deaf, and hearing individuals all interact to form a unique learning environment. Because of this environment the larger Rochester community is known nationally, and especially among the Deaf community, as a place where Deaf culture, and Deaf, deaf, and hard of hearing individuals all thrive. Also, things like making an appointment to see a doctor are often easier for people living in this community because the larger Rochester community has adapted to having a large Deaf community living within its city. These and other offices are often, although not always, more socially and technologically advanced in terms of interacting with members of the Deaf community than other places in the U.S. This culture or climate makes Rochester a unique place to investigate and to gather information about college educated deaf women's work experiences.

Somewhat in contrast to this, Boston, Massachusetts is a larger metropolitan city, also in the northeast, with a sizable deaf population due to the many schools, hospitals and resources that exist in such a large city. However, there are no official Deaf colleges in this city and perhaps due to the size and cultural diversity of the city, the Deaf community, while definitely thriving, seems somewhat more displaced than in Rochester. Among the Deaf community, Boston is known as a reasonable place to live overall; however, Deaf individuals often run into different obstacles when calling to make doctors appointments and go about their everyday lives. This may be because, unlike Rochester, the Deaf community in Boston is less concentrated and more spread out among the city. Despite having set up the study in this way, there were not overwhelming differences in the lives of these deaf women that seemed based solely on geographical location. At the end of this chapter, I have included a brief summary of each respondent's life.

The Research Process

After obtaining names of potential respondents from personal and professional contacts, I emailed these women telling them about myself and my wish to interview ten Deaf, deaf, and hard of hearing mothers, who had worked for pay, were college educated or had some college experience, and were approximately forty to sixty years old. The rationale for focusing on college educated women ages forty to sixty was that one would think that being college educated and older would let these women have an advantage and be working for pay. As stated earlier, my decision to interview this particular group of deaf women also emerged from the fieldwork experiences of working with a deaf woman and her family to tell her life history and as a result of discussions with researchers at NTID who are looking into similar issues (S. Foster & J. MacLeod-Gallinger, personal communication, March 21, 2002). I also included in this email a bit about myself and how having a Deaf brother as well as my fieldwork experience had influenced my decision to pursue this as a topic of research. Many of the women seemed willing to talk to me either because they trusted the person who gave me their name, because I had a brother who is Deaf and a shared understanding of the Deaf community, or a combination of both. In this way, I had a certain "insider" status, which allowed me a unique access to this community.

In my initial email to potential respondents, I was up front about my knowing Sign Exact English (SEE), but not American Sign Language (ASL). Some members of the Deaf community view SEE as an attempt of hearing and some deaf educators to colonize them by taking their native language, ASL, and making it more like spoken English (Lane, 1999). In SEE every word and tense is signed, whereas in ASL, words are communicated through a variety of signs, body postures, and facial expressions, markers that make it a distinct language. Putting this in a context, in the 1970s when I learned sign language, schools were teaching Deaf and hearing people SEE in an effort to integrate the Deaf into a hearing society (Baynton, 1996). Thus, by learning SEE, I, in some ways, have been part of the larger system of oppression that works against the Deaf community.

To deal with this issue, after consulting with my contacts in the Deaf community, I decided to give the option to the women to have a sign language interpreter present for our interviews. One hearing researcher, who works with members of the Deaf community, went so far as to say that the information that I would get without a sign language interpreter would not be "valid" (S. Foster, personal communication, March 21, 2002). Without the use of an interpreter, she argued, respondents would tend to simplify their language and not elaborate as much if they did not have someone to interpret their story. Although I somewhat disagree with this sentiment, I decided to have the women of the study to make this decision. Also, since I was interested in how the women made decisions about their language and how their languages shifted in various contexts, I wanted to understand how and why they made these decisions. I offered to pay for the interpreter as well as to hire interpreters who my respondents either had a preference for or to hire interpreters that did not live and work in the area where my respondents resided in an effort to protect their confidentiality. Beth was the only woman in my study who requested an ASL interpreter. The interpreter, Hannah, was a close personal friend and colleague of Beth's with whom she works at NTID. Also, Ellen, who did not request an interpreter, had her husband stay for the interview. Despite his also being Deaf and a native ASL speaker, I could understand him somewhat better than Ellen. As if anticipating this, they had arranged for him to be there.

These two instances of a third person who acted as an interpreter posed interesting challenges as well as dynamics to these interviews. For example, in Beth's interview, there were times when the interpreter asked to "step out of her role as the interpreter" and added, usually with Beth's permission, a commentary on the subject. This struck me as unusual as interpreters do not typically do this; however, my respondent who was also friends with the interpreter, gave her permission, so, in this case, I trusted her judgment. Likewise, in Ellen's interview, there were times when her husband commented on the subject at hand, such as deaf education programs in Massachusetts. In these two cases, there were also times where Hannah or Peter, due to their personal relationships with the respondents, prompted Beth and Ellen to share a particular story or elaborate on something. In this way, these two individuals also acted, at times, as interviewers in these settings. Although somewhat inconsistent with the format of the other eight interviews, the dynamics of these two individuals in these cases enhanced and also shaped the information that I gathered from these two women.

They also were invaluable in helping me to establish rapport with these two respondents; however, there were also times where this dynamic challenged how I "traditionally" built rapport with the women. For example, when Hannah or Peter interpreted what I was saying, Beth and Ellen would look at them and not me. Thus, despite me signing (in SEE), overly enunciating my words in an effort to make for better lip reading, nodding, smiling, and making eye contact with Beth or Ellen, since they were watching the interpreter or husband, I was unsure of how well I was building rapport with each of them. In Beth's interview, I brought this up as a point of discussion and Beth told me that she could see me out of the corner of her eye. She said that I did not need to sign, but could if I wanted to do so. In this way, these two interviews challenged me as a researcher to think about how I would establish rapport with respondents and to somewhat modify my strategies to more effectively develop this rapport.

In my initial email to respondents, I also asked if they would agree to be both audio and visually recorded in our interviews. Both Bogdan and Biklen (1998) and Taylor and Bogdan (1998) discuss this qualitative method in terms of visual recording, mostly in the form of photographs. As there exists little sociological research on how to use video cameras effectively in interviews, I negotiated the logistics of this as I conducted my study. In an effort to capture the languages of these deaf women more fully, I set the video camera on them while I sat behind the camera. I placed an additional audio recorder in the middle of the room between us as a backup. Stephanie was one woman in this study who specifically requested that I not audio record our conversation. As a native ASL speaker and Deaf woman, she explained that she would prefer not to be audio recorded because she would not use her voice when speaking with me, however, she would use mouth movements and gestures along with her native language, ASL. All of the other women in this study were audio as well as video taped.

As Taylor and Bogdan (1998) advise, often the use of pseudonyms is best to ensure that no harm will come to respondents. Sometimes, however, respondents, especially in life history research, wish to use their real name. I decided, for issues of confidentiality, to use pseudonyms for all of my respondents. I made this decision because the Deaf community is known to be a close knit community. It is not uncommon for people within this community to personally know or know of people across the country through Deaf clubs, schools for the deaf, and through friends and family members. By giving the women pseudonyms, it would minimize the risk of having the women or one of their family members recognized and possibly ostracized for things said in our interviews about their lives or the Deaf community. In an effort to make this group of women visible for perhaps the first time to some, I did, however, leave their biographies fairly close to their lives, so that readers could get a fuller account of their experiences and struggles. If one of the deaf women in my study later expresses interest in having her real name used in publications or possibly in co-presenting at a conference and thus revealing her identity, then I will have a conversation with my respondent about the pros and cons of this. So far, no woman has requested this. Teresa requested that I give her a copy of the video tape from our interview, which I did at the end of this study, as she is interested in writing a book on the story of her life.

As Taylor and Bogdan (1998) point out, one of the easier ways to get respondents is to use the "snowballing" technique where you get to know respondents and then they introduce you to other possible respondents. After speaking with my initial contacts and with some who agreed to an interview, I asked them to refer me to friends, relatives, and acquaintances who might also like to participate in an interview. This worked quite well and all of the women that I interviewed seemed eager to tell the stories of their lives. Virtually everyone that I contacted agreed to an interview. Only one woman, due to a conflict that arose with her children's schedule and our interview, did not show up for an interview.

Snowball sampling, although an effective way to gain access to respondents, often leads to a sample which can lack in diversity as we often "typically" think of diversity. Generally speaking, the women in my study referred me to other women who were similar to them in terms of race and social class. Part of this was also due to the way I structured this study. By seeking women who were college educated, this often meant deaf women who were white and middle class or as they self-identified, "economically comfortable." Also, by contacting respondents through email, this presumed certain things about their social class in that they would have the resources to have a personal computer. Despite these issues, I sought to expand our sociological ideas about diversity to include and illustrate the differences *within* this group of deaf women. Thus, in my analysis, I draw particular attention to their language(s), where they grew up, if they were raised in the oral tradition, manual tradition or a combination of both, and how they saw themselves as deaf, Deaf, hard of hearing, or somewhere in between. I also sought to gather information about how these women conceptualized deafness in terms of it being a disability, linguistic minority, or ethnicity. In this way, the women in this study who represent a particular group of deaf women also vary enormously in these experiences and definitions.

In these semi-structured, open ended, and active interviews, I began with conversation starters.[2] These included a discussion of my study and my interest in deaf women and work. Also, at the beginning of each interview, as well as throughout, we negotiated how we would communicate. I sometimes took notes in the interviews, but usually did not as it was challenging to write and sign at the same time. When transcribing, I relied on the audio and video tapes as well as my memory of the interviews. After working to establish rapport, I then asked respondents questions about their educational experiences and moved on to discussions about their first jobs. Next, I asked them to construct a chronology of their jobs. I then posed questions regarding their relationships with their partners and children to ask how these experiences have affected their daily lives.

In May 2003, after phase one of my data collection, I sent all respondents a Mother's Day card, which also included a letter updating them on the progress of the study.[3] As many of these women described feeling isolated in various settings, I wrote this letter in an effort to keep them informed and connected to the study as well as to invite collaboration on some of my findings. I also saw it as another way to build rapport. In this letter, I let them know that I would be contacting them soon for follow-up interviews. As stated earlier, in the spirit of being flexible, I then conducted these follow-up interviews with the women to gain a fuller understanding of their educational, family, and work experiences.[4] In these interviews, I had a series of questions which asked them to comment on some of the major themes, as I saw them emerging from the study, as well as to answer some demographical questions about themselves. I also included a section for each individual woman where I asked them to clarify various questions from our first interview. There was also a space for them to add anything else that they felt might contribute to our knowledge about the experiences of college educated deaf women. In all of these interviews, I paid particular attention to the obstacles that they faced, while also working to note places where they resisted these obstacles.

Nine of the ten women participated in follow-up interviews, which were all conducted over email. Ellen, the one woman who did not take part in the follow-up interview, told me that her computer had crashed and that she would contact me at a later time. Despite repeated attempts to contact her, I got no response. It is perhaps telling that Ellen did not respond to my request. She was the one woman in this study who did not finish college, she seemed to be "somewhat economically comfortable," and her husband, although not necessarily asked, was present for the interview. She was also probably the strongest ASL speaker in my study as she did not use her voice in our interview and had a strong Deaf identity. Her refusal to participate in the follow-up interview might have something to do with her social class standing as well as her strong identity as a Deaf woman. Researchers have commented on how working class or "somewhat economically comfortable" women are often reluctant participants in research since they are often criticized for their actions (Reinharz, 1992). There is also evidence that some researchers have allegedly taken advantage of people who might speak a language other than their own, which has led to a distrust of researchers (de Cristoforo, 1987). In this case, despite my offering to pay for a sign language interpreter, Ellen's husband, Peter, acted as one at various points in our interview. This suggests that perhaps there were issues of trust involved, on account of my being a researcher and non native ASL speaker, despite my "insider" knowledge of the Deaf community from the experience of having a Deaf brother. Despite all of this, Ellen was one of the most welcoming women that I interviewed as she let me hold her young daughter and invited me to stay after the interview for a cup of coffee and her homemade coffee cake, which she also packaged for me to take on my trip home.

After each interview was completed, I transcribed both the audio and video tapes and coded each interview with relevant themes. I also wrote extensive observer comments within my transcriptions where I tried to situate myself in the research process. Since transcribing these particular tapes involved knowing sign language, I transcribed all of the tapes except for the audio tape of Beth's interview where an interpreter was involved. For this tape, as with the others, however, I went back and watched the video tape and transcribed Beth's gestures, mouth movements, pauses, and the places where she used sign language, but the interpreter did not interpret. I also edited the places where there were mistakes in what was transcribed. For all of these interviews, I proceeded with this double and sometimes triple method of transcribing. I would transcribe in spoken English, ASL (where I could translate), SEE, gestures, mouth movements, silences, and writings between us. After an initial coding of relevant themes, I went back and recoded by hand and established twelve major themes, which I listed and kept with me as I reread and "rewatched" the data. I highlighted the themes in different colors on the interview transcripts as well as developed an index card system for each theme and wrote down where these themes occurred, if at all, in each women's interview where I kept a filing system of my data.

For each respondent, I then made an "interview summary," which consisted of each woman's demographic information as well as a timeline for their family, education, and work experiences. The interview summaries also included a description of how the interview proceeded and how each woman told the story of their life. I did this in an effort to organize their life histories on their terms. Next, for each respondent, I made a "life chronology" of their story. In an effort to organize their lives into stages where I could make some claims in my analysis, I identified five life phases, which included "early life," "teenage years," "college years," "after college years," and "later life/present" experiences. Within each of these five life phases, I listed two categories and provided descriptions for their "education and work experiences" as well as their "family experiences" during each of these five phases of their lives. Next, I went back and recoded the "life chronologies" and "interview summaries" noting additional emerging themes.

After the follow-up interviews, I followed this same method for coding and transcribing and then edited the life chronologies and interview summaries to reflect this new and updated information. Finally, since I noticed that there were differences in some of the themes due to geography, I developed cards for each woman with a brief update of their demographics, family, educational, and work experiences and arranged them by the Rochester women and Boston women on a bulletin board. During this process, I also periodically watched selected clips from the women's interviews while also rereading my interview transcripts. I was able to code over 600 pages of single spaced data. My previous fieldwork on the life history of a Deaf woman, which included similar themes as the women in this study and led to this investigation, consisted of a total of over 430 pages of single spaced data. Thus, the total for this entire project included 1,030 pages of single spaced data.

DATA ANALYSIS

I began my data analysis with the daily experiences of these college educated deaf women in their paid and unpaid work lives while also considering their educational and family histories. Since I sought to ground the analysis in their words, I tried to use the women's language as major themes whenever possible. All of the women spoke of being "lifetime educators" and "self-advocates" in their family, educational, mothering, and paid work experiences and how this shaped their identities. After investigating how they carved out places for themselves in these various locales, I began to see how their career opportunities and experiences in the hearing world were often limited. Despite being educated orally, many of these women chose or were tracked into working at schools for the deaf or in the deaf world. It seemed that in order for them to succeed in their hearing work places, they were often faced with making political decisions about their identities as deaf women.

While I continued analyzing my data, I used Glaser and Strauss' (1967) constant comparative method where I worked to collect and analyze data at the same time. This allowed me, as mentioned earlier, to later follow up with the women on emerging themes in the data in our follow-up interviews. Like others who have done life history research, I did this in an effort to make the data analysis more of a collaborative effort between respondents and myself (Shostak, 1983). This seemed to work well as the women all appeared to be committed to telling the story of their lives. Also, the college educated deaf woman with whom I did life history research with prior to this study, as well as a deaf colleague of mine, served as informal consultants on my analysis. I tried to strike a balance then between directly involving the women of this study in the process of analysis while being careful to not take advantage of their volunteered and often limited time.

THE WRITING PROCESS

As I began writing and furthering my analysis, I was faced with making major decisions about how to re-present the stories of these women. My transcripts are filled with instances where the women as well as I slip in and out of ASL, SEE, use mouth movements, silences, gestures, finger spelling, writing out words, and where the two of us go back and forth to understand particular words. To make my analysis more readable, I have edited their words and mine so as to not make their quotations too lengthy. When the women use ASL grammar I have tried, whenever possible, to preserve their language as is. This may or may not trip up the reader while making sense of my analysis; however, I chose to do this for two reasons. First, I wanted to keep some of the flavor of our interviews intact to illustrate how, through our "talk," we negotiated what it meant to be deaf, hearing, or somewhere in between. Second, since this is a group of women who has not been written about, I thought it important that the story of their lives reflect their native language of ASL, despite it being a written and not visual account.

BIOGRAPHIES OF THE WOMEN

Although there were not overwhelming differences between the groups of Rochester and Boston women, there were indeed some differences that are noteworthy. First, while all of the Rochester women's current or most recent jobs were working at a school or college for the deaf, only two of the Boston women are currently in this situation. This may be due, in part, to the large Deaf community, NTID, and various schools for the deaf which are part of the Rochester area. Second, while all of the Rochester women currently work full-time, with the exception of Teresa whose children have families of their own and is retired, only two of the Boston women work full-time while the other three are stay-at-home mothers. This is perhaps partly due to the Rochester women being a slightly older cohort whose ages ranged from thirty-eight to sixty-three while the Boston women's ages ranged from ages thirty-four to thirty-nine. Thirdly, while all of the

Rochester women described their family's economic status as economically comfortable, only two of the Boston women described their families in this way while the other three Boston women described their families as somewhat economically comfortable. Finally, although none of the Rochester women spoke of feeling socially isolated, three of the Boston women, expressed feeling somewhat isolated in their all hearing communities, which suggests that living in a place such as Rochester where there is a large Deaf community may influence these women's experiences and sense of themselves. What follows is a brief description of each respondent with a profile of their life history.

Rochester Women

Beth[5]:

Beth is a Deaf, 41-year-old, white, economically comfortable Assistant Professor at NTID. She is also a mother of two hearing children and married, yet separated from her husband who is hard of hearing and also works at NTID. Her daughter is fourteen and her son is nine. Beth comes from an all hearing family with an older brother and sister. Her parents, who divorced shortly after they discovered she was deaf at age two, are both college educated. Her father is the owner of several different companies while her mother, who immigrated to America, worked as an executive administrative assistant. When her parents found out that she was deaf, her mother bought a sign language book and took it home to teach her sign. Thus, Beth stated that she was raised as a manualist and still considers herself a manualist today. When we communicated, Beth did not use her voice, but she did use mouth movements and sign. In this interview, we had the assistance of an interpreter, Hannah. When Beth spoke to me with the assistance of this certified sign language interpreter, she used ASL, but when Hannah was not present, she used SEE so that I could better understand her story.

From ages two until sixteen, Beth attended and commuted to a manual state residential school for the deaf in her home state. She then went to public school for one year where she was the only deaf person and had no interpreters or note takers. After her mother's job transfer, for the last two years of her high school experience, she attended a school for the deaf on the campus of Gallaudet. She attended Gallaudet for one semester, but then transferred to NTID where she majored in Business for two years. After changing majors a few times, she got her Associate's degree in Mechanical Art in 1985. She then got her BFA from RIT/NTID. Next, she worked on her MA in ASL Linguistics at a local hearing college, but then decided to go back to RIT/NTID where she completed her MS in ASL teaching.

Beth began her career working in the printing profession in various darkrooms and doing typesetting. After these experiences, she worked as a graphic designer for six years at NTID until she was laid off. For the next three years, she worked as a teacher at NTID teaching deaf students. As part of an internship experience, she also worked for a local school for the deaf teaching students in grades K-12 and then stayed working there in a paid position. Currently, she works at NTID in a tenure track position as an Assistant Professor.

Kristen:

Kristen is a Deaf, 38-year-old, Catholic, white, economically comfortable Counselor and teacher at NTID. She is also the mother of two deaf children and married to her deaf husband who, self-employed, sells life insurance. He is able to work out of the home and also be there for their son who is ten and daughter who is eight. Kristen comes from an all hearing family with one older brother. Raised as an oralist, her father, a chemical engineer, and her mother, a homemaker, encouraged her to talk. Although she did learn ASL from deaf adults at night while staying at the oral school she attended from ages three through five, she stopped using it again until she was twenty when she attended NTID. Currently, Kristen, who signs, also uses a method of communication called "cued speech" where phonetics and pronunciation are emphasized. She is also teaching it to her two children. When Kristen and I communicated, she used her voice as well as sign and English word order.

Kristen, who originally thought that she was born hearing, has recently discovered that she has the "deaf gene" and was deaf at birth. From ages one until two, she attended a hearing school and a Montessori school two times a week. Due to her father's job transfer, she and her family moved to another state, where she was enrolled and lived at an oral state residential school for the deaf from ages two until eight. She attended an elementary school for one year which used "total communication" methods so that she could get a smooth transition from her deaf oral school to a hearing school. Then, due to the passing of Public Law 94–142 in 1975, legislation which led to children with "disabilities" being part of public and private schools, from the third through seventh grade, she attended a private, religious hearing school. She had no interpreters and asked friends for copies of their notes. After skipping eighth grade, she attended a private, religious, hearing high school with no interpreters. She attended a small, all women's, hearing college for two years where she had no interpreters and again asked friends for copies of their notes. Kristen then transferred to NTID and in 1985 got her BA in Social Work. She completed her education by getting her MA in Social Work through a nine month accelerated program at a large, all hearing university. She had a friend, who was a note taker at another college, volunteer to take notes for her. She had an interpreter, but the "quality" was different from that at the deaf and hard of hearing college. Also, although Vocational Rehabilitation Services paid for some of these services, she also had to pay for the difference.

Kristen describes her first job experience at the age of twelve when she worked for the United Way with children who have cerebral palsy. She worked as a babysitter from ages fourteen through fifteen and for a temporary agency doing filing work from ages fifteen through eighteen. In the last summer of her senior year in high school, she worked for the post office. Other work experience includes an internship as part of her MA program as a social worker for a local social services agency where she helped parents who were deaf and also had another disability to develop their parenting skills when raising their hearing children. Next, she worked at an alcohol treatment center for five years with deaf individuals struggling with alcoholism. Kristen's next position was a two year temporary position as Counselor at NTID. She then worked in another administrative office at NTID for four years. Currently, she works at NTID doing her old position as a Counselor as well as teaches a freshman seminar.

Janice:

Janice is a Deaf, 47-year-old, Jewish, economically comfortable Director at a manual residential school for the deaf and mother of two deaf children. Her son is eighteen and her daughter is fifteen. She is married to a deaf man who works at NTID. Janice grew up in an all deaf family. Her brother is older than she by two years. Her grandparents on her father's side are also deaf. Growing up, her family used ASL, but they used English word order and her parents wanted her to be an oralist. Her parents were somewhat ashamed of being deaf; however, their views have changed. Her mother, who immigrated to America from Germany when she was eleven, did not attend college. Her father, although he was accepted to a hearing college, did not attend. Although Janice was raised as an oralist, I would say that she is a manualist because of how she primarily signed and did not use her voice. She did (I believe for my benefit) use English grammar instead of ASL. She considers ASL to be her "first language."

From 1956–1972, Janice attended an oral residential school for the deaf from ages two until seventeen where she lived at the school for a time. Her family specifically moved to this state so that she and her brother could attend this oral school. Next, she attended Gallaudet University for four years and got her BA through the School of Education majoring in Social

Work and Psychology in 1976. After two years, she got her MA in Elementary Education in 1978, also from Gallaudet. Currently, Janice is working on her Certificate in Education Administration at a local hearing college where she is the only deaf student.

After getting her MA degree, Janice worked at a school teaching elementary education for six years. After this, she was a stay-at-home mom for five years. For the last one or two years of staying at home with her children, she worked part-time as a teacher for the deaf at a public school and then worked as a preschool teacher. After moving to Rochester, Janice worked in an administrative office at NTID from 1991–1993 at eighty percent time. Next, she got a job at a residential school for the deaf as a Coordinator and worked in that position from 1993–1999. She currently is a Director at this same school and has been since 1999.

Stephanie:

Stephanie is a Deaf, 45-year-old, Catholic, white, economically comfortable ASL Specialist at a manual residential school for the deaf, where Janice also works, and mother of three hearing children. She also works by contract as a deaf blind interpreter and as an interpreter at her daughter's school. Her first daughter is sixteen, followed by her second daughter who is fourteen, and her son who is eleven. She is married to a deaf man who works at NTID. Stephanie's parents are hearing and she has five older sisters and one older brother. All of her siblings are hearing except for one of Stephanie's sisters who is closest to her in age and older than her by two years. Her parents, who pushed oral communication in the home, both left school in the eighth grade and worked as farmers. Stephanie is a manualist who asked me not to tape record our interview since she does not use her voice. She used sign and mouth movements when speaking to me and switched back from English (for my benefit) to ASL grammar. There were only a few points in the interview when she did use her voice and that was to clarify something that I still could not understand after her third or fourth time signing it.

Stephanie, who grew up oral, went to public schools from the ages of three until thirteen. At this time, in the 1950s, the term "mainstreaming" was not used; however, she was in a "special class" for the deaf while she also had some classes with similar experiences to those who were later labeled as mainstreamed. She then went to a manual state residential school for the deaf in her home area and lived there from sixth through twelfth grade. This school used manual methods as well as "total communication." After two years of working, she attended Gallaudet for five years and graduated in 1993 with her BA in Communication Arts or Deaf Studies.

From 1997–1999 she did some graduate work in Secondary Education at NTID.

While she was at the manual state residential school for the deaf, she worked as a manager of a small store for four years. She also worked with the preschool children at this school. After graduating from this school, she worked as the only deaf person doing clerical work in an insurance company. As part of her undergraduate experience, she did a six month internship in India where she worked with deaf adults as a Regional Interpreter. After graduating with her BA, she worked for Gallaudet for eight years as a Coordinator in an administrative office. While raising her children, she worked part-time by contracts in the area as an interpreter. Currently, she has been working full-time the past two months as an ASL Specialist at a manual state residential school for the deaf and continues to work by contract as a deaf blind interpreter and as an interpreter at her daughter's school.

Teresa:

Teresa is a Deaf, 63-year-old, Southern Baptist, white, economically comfortable retired college teacher and editor of a deaf magazine. She has three hearing children, which include her son who is thirty-seven, her daughter who is thirty-six, and her daughter who is thirty-two. She also has three hearing grandchildren. Her husband is a deaf engineer who most recently worked as a professor at NTID. Teresa comes from an all hearing family and has a brother who is three years younger than she and a sister who is five years younger than she. Her father, a Baptist minister, and her mother, who worked as the principal of the Vacation Bible School at the church, encouraged Teresa to talk. Thus, she was raised as an oralist and says that she is "not a native" speaker of ASL. She first learned sign language in college in her late teens and then again when she began working at NTID. When Teresa spoke to me, she used her voice as well as sign. She used English word order; however, there were instances when she mixed in ASL phrases or words.

After her parents found out that she was deaf, they took her to the state residential school for the deaf in their home Southern state; however, a woman that worked there recommended that since Teresa could talk and lip read, the family should send her to an oral state residential school for the deaf, which was also a teacher's training college in the Midwest. Thus, the family moved to this state so that Teresa could attend school there. She attended this school, which forbade sign language, from preschool until the eighth grade while living at home. Then, for two years, she attended a public hearing school where she was the only deaf student in her class and had no interpreters or note takers. In an effort to be with her grandparents and cousin, she moved back to her home southern state and attended the last two years of her high school education in a public high school without interpreters or note takers. From there she attended a small, all women's hearing college in the south and got her BA in Home Economics. Again, she did not have interpreters or note takers in college. Later in her life, Teresa went back to school and received her MA in Women's Studies at a state university in 1995.

Teresa describes her first job experience as a teacher for the first all deaf class at her father's church Vacation Bible School program where she orally taught a small group of students bible studies. Her next job, at age eighteen, was in the summer after her first year of college where she worked as one of four deaf students on a student staff of four hundred at a church conference center in the south cleaning out dormitories for conference participants. After she received her BA, she worked as the first deaf teacher at the oral state residential school for the deaf that she attended as a child. Here she taught Home Economics and Gym, but did not have a "real classroom." Later, after she got married and had children, she worked part-time in her father's church office. Although she was not paid, an important part of her work history is when she and her husband ran a volunteer TTY business out of their home where they sold TTYs to deaf people in the community. During this time, she and three other women also formed an organization for deaf women in the Rochester community and put on various workshops and conferences. Also, during this time Teresa worked for twenty-two years at NTID where her husband also worked. She began as the first and only deaf secretary and worked there for ten years. Later, she did this job part-time as well as taught a course part-time. Also, she was the editor for six years of a local deaf newsletter. Currently, Teresa, who retired from teaching three years ago and from her editor position recently, still volunteers her time for the newsletter and the deaf women's group.

Boston Women

Carol:

Carol is a Deaf, 39-year-old, Catholic, white, economically comfortable Assistant Controller at a manual state residential school for the deaf. She also teaches ASL to parents and siblings of people in the outside community. Carol is married to a deaf man who, after being laid off twice from graphic design positions, works part-time at the same school doing graphic arts for their newsletters and other publications. They have one six-year-old daughter who is hearing. Carol comes from an all hearing family with one sister who is two years younger and one brother who is four years younger. Her mother, who was trained as a teacher, got into deaf education when she learned of her daughter's deafness and became the Director of the oral state residential school for the deaf where Carol attended elementary school. Her father worked as a chemical engineer. Both of her parents went to college. Carol, raised as an oralist, used English grammar when she spoke to me instead of ASL (most likely for my benefit). She mentioned that she does know and prefer ASL. She first learned sign when her mother took her to sign language classes before she went to elementary school and then again when she went to NTID. During our interview, there were times where Carol signed something, but did not verbalize it, which suggests that she does indeed prefer ASL.

From preschool to second grade, Carol attended an oral state residential school for the deaf in her hometown. She then went to public school in her hometown from second grade until high school. Next, she went to NTID where she graduated in two years with her Associate's degree in Business. She began working on her BA in Marketing Research at RIT; however, due to deaths in her family, she moved back home and did not finish her degree.

Carol's first work experience was at an electric company in an all hearing office. This job was part of her co-op requirement for her Associate's degree. After college and since 1988, she has worked as the Assistant Controller at a manual state residential school for the deaf where she is the "only one deaf in administration." She also supervises a hearing woman in this capacity. As stated, she also teaches ASL part-time to parents and siblings of people in the outside community.

Heather:

Heather is a deaf, 36-year-old, white, somewhat economically comfortable Statistics Analyst and Programmer at a large hearing university and mother of two hearing sons ages nine and five. She is recently divorced from her deaf husband who works as a drafting operator. Heather's parents are both hearing and both went to college. Her father is a programmer and her mother is a nurse. She is the oldest of three children. Her middle brother is hearing, and her younger brother by three years is also deaf. Her oldest brother and parents do not know sign and she grew up as an oralist. She learned sign in her second year of college after transferring to NTID. When we spoke, Heather spoke and signed in English grammatical order.

After her parents found out that she was deaf at age one, they enrolled her at age three in the first class of an all deaf preschool, which is housed at a hearing college in the city. She attended this preschool with Debbie from this study. After this experience, Heather went to a preschool in her hometown for two years, which had a program for the deaf. At age five, she was mainstreamed in her hometown's public school system until she was eighteen and graduated in 1985. During this experience, she had no interpreters, she did have two note takers, and she did not know sign language. After high school, she attended a small hearing college in another state for one and a half years. She did not have interpreters and asked her friends for their notes. Heather transferred to RIT and got her BA in Biology in 1989 and her MA in Statistics from RIT in 1992.

Heather's first job was when she was age seventeen and she worked in a nursing home as a dietary aide in the kitchen setting up plates for residents. She worked part-time at a fast food restaurant the summer after her first year in college. While working on her BA, she tutored students part-time for biology, math, chemistry, and physics. In the summer of 1988, as part of her co-op experience for her BA, she lived on the campus of Gallaudet while working for the government doing data entry. After she graduated with her BA, she moved to another state and worked as a researcher for fourteen months in a biology lab. Next, she moved back to Rochester and worked part-time in a medical lab while looking for a job. While working on her MA, she worked for ten months at RIT tutoring deaf students who were taking courses at the hearing college. Her next job was as a Research Assistant for three years studying DNA at a large hearing university in her home state. Currently, she is a Statistics Analyst and Programmer, where she has worked for seven years at this same large hearing university.

Ellen:

Ellen is a Deaf, 34-year-old, white, somewhat economically comfortable stay-at-home mother who also works part-time teaching ASL in a family sign program. She was married to a deaf man from 1997 until they divorced in 2000. Currently, she is married to a deaf man who works for the government and they have two daughters. The oldest is two and deaf (technically hard of hearing) and the youngest is six weeks old and deaf. Ellen grew up with hearing parents who worked full-time running a family locksmith business. They did not attend college. She has four older brothers and one younger sister. All of her siblings are hearing except the second oldest brother who is also deaf. Growing up, Ellen mentioned that her family did sign, but that it was mostly "home signs." She grew up oral, but from interacting with her, I would say she is a manualist as she rarely used her voice and relied heavily on sign with an emphasis on ASL grammar. She mentioned that she prefers ASL.

From ages four until sixteen, she attended an oral state residential school for the deaf in her home state, but not in her hometown. In her junior and senior years in high school, she was mainstreamed in a public high school outside of her hometown where she had interpreters and a note taker. After working for a while, she moved to the Midwest with her first husband and worked part-time at a technical college on her teaching degree; however, after her divorce, she moved back to her home state and did not finish her degree.

Ellen's work experience included working in a factory for five years in various different positions where she was the only deaf employee. During her time in the Midwest and while she working on her college degree, she taught ASL to Chinese couples. Currently, she is a full-time stay-at-home mother and also works part-time at night teaching ASL in a family sign program.

Debbie:

Debbie is a Deaf, 39-year-old, Catholic, white somewhat economically comfortable stay-at-home mother of two hearing children. Her son is ten and her daughter is six. She also volunteers her time as a Systems Analyst for a consulting company as well as volunteers on the board of directors of a Deaf organization. She is married to a hearing man who is a non practicing lawyer and now works as a Director for a small company. He signs to her as well as speaks when they communicate. Debbie comes from an all hearing family with a sister who is one year younger than her and a brother who is three years younger than she. When her mother, who was trained and worked as a public school teacher, found out that Debbie was deaf, she got into deaf education and was a trustee of a school that Debbie later attended. She also did lots of volunteer work. Her father is an insurance broker and was also on the board of an oral state residential school for the deaf. Debbie was raised as an oralist. She does have a "sign name" or one that she uses when speaking with members of the Deaf community, but when she talks to me, she signs, uses her voice, and English grammar. Of all the respondents, Debbie was probably the easiest for me to understand as she had "good" speech.

From ages three through six, she attended, along with Heather, the first class of an all deaf preschool, which is housed at a hearing college in the city. She then went to public school for a time, but it did not work out, so her parents enrolled her in an oral state residential school for the deaf from ages seven to eleven. After that, she went to a small, private hearing school until the ninth grade. Then, from tenth grade to twelfth grade she went to another private hearing school and graduated in 1982. Debbie then got her BA in Psychology in 1986 from a small, religiously affiliated liberal arts, hearing college in her home state. She was the only deaf student at the college and did not have interpreters until the last semester her senior year when she could not understand a professor. Next, Debbie received her BSBA or a degree in Business Administration in Management Information Systems at a large, urban, hearing college. She had interpreters at this college. Finally, she received her MBA after attending a small, hearing, business college from 1993–1994. She was the first deaf student to attend this college and the only deaf student at the time so she had to "educate them" on the services that she needed and was able to get interpreters and the necessary support.

Debbie began her career by working full-time as an Accountant while working on her BSBA degree. For the next four years, she worked for an investment company doing quality control and then systems development and programming. She had a temporary job for one month doing administrative work before she became a Business Analyst and Part Time Manager where she supervised a team of people. As her children grew up, she worked "part time" from home, then full-time when her daughter was in day care, then part-time again to take care of her children and eventually gave up her manager responsibilities. She then worked in business where she negotiated for part-time, but was laid off. Currently, she is a full-time stay-at-home mother and volunteers as a Systems Analyst for a consulting company as well as volunteers on the board of directors of a Deaf organization.

Marie:

Marie is a Deaf, 38-year-old, Lutheran, white, economically comfortable full-time stay-at-home mother. She also volunteers her time to help her father-in-law with the filing, paperwork, and taxes for his convenience store chain business. She has four hearing children. Her daughter is ten, her son is eight, her next son is four, and her youngest son is eighteen months. She is married to a hard of hearing man who also works for the family's convenience store chain business. Marie comes from an all hearing family where she is the sixth of seven children. Her father was a plumber and her mother was a housewife who also worked in the medical records office at a hospital. They did not attend college, but all of her siblings did. She states that her parents were "very strong about me speaking" and had her do speech therapy. She was raised as an oralist and does not rely heavily on sign language. When I asked her if she had a sign name, she said that she did not really have one. Marie learned a few signs in the fifth grade and in junior high from watching her interpreter, but she learned more signs when she went to NTID. When speaking with me, she used English grammar and was fairly easy for me to understand.

From preschool until the sixth grade Marie attended a public school outside of her hometown because they had a special program for the deaf. She went to the junior high in this same town and was separated from the hearing kids in a deaf program. Then, after negotiating with her parents, the town, and another deaf student in her town, she attended the public high school in her hometown for four years. Despite not wanting one, she also had a teacher for the deaf at this school. She then went to NTID and graduated with her Associate's degree in Data Processing. Next, she went to RIT for three years and got her BS in Information Systems.

Marie describes her first job as when she was in high school working in a nursing home in the cleaning department. Next, as part of her AAS degree, she had a co-op job for six months at a hospital in her home state working in the computer department. Then, she had another co-op job for six months in a Midwest state working for a national organization for the deaf in computer relations. After graduating with her BS, she worked for two years at an insurance company writing computer programs for the statistical department. Next, she worked for a software company for seven years in the Purchasing Department doing computer programming and analysis. Currently, she is a full-time stay-at-home mother. As stated, she also volunteers her time to help her father-in-law with the filing, paperwork, and taxes for his convenience store chain business. Finally, she also volunteers as a Girl Scout Troop leader for her daughter's troop.

CONCLUSION

The following chapters explore the family, educational, mothering, and paid work experiences in the lives of these college educated deaf women. The first data chapter unpacks how these women negotiated their identities in both oral and manual schools as well as in their early family experiences and personal relationships. The second data chapter describes their mothering and activist work. It illustrates how they make decisions about communication in their current families and how these decisions affect their own senses of themselves as college educated deaf women. The third data chapter focuses on the relationship between their paid work experiences and how they balanced that with their mothering and activism. It uncovers how these women are often tracked or make the decision to work in the deaf world due to a desire to communicate more easily with their colleagues. The final chapter offers a discussion of the paid and unpaid work experiences of these college educated deaf women as well as implications for the future with respect to educational processes and hiring procedures.

Chapter Three
Family, Educational Experiences, and Relationships

Through their early family and educational experiences, these deaf women negotiated their own identities and places for themselves in relation to both the Deaf and hearing worlds. All of the women experienced a type of cultural shift either when they attended a college for the deaf or were exposed to the Deaf community and learned American Sign Language (ASL). These experiences led the women to continually assess their options, develop strategies, and eventually find places for themselves. How they, along with their families, thought of themselves as deaf shaped their educational opportunities.

How these families discovered or acknowledged their daughter's deafness is critical to understanding how these deaf women thought of themselves as part of the deaf or hearing worlds. Also, parents' decisions about the girl's educations became a key factor for these deaf women because decisions about educating their daughters orally, manually, or both influenced how these women thought of themselves. Various factors such as parents' resistance to "expert" advice, how they taught their daughters at home, and how they became involved in deaf education played a role in their decisions about their daughter's educations. Their stories also show how deaf education became privatized, in some ways, as a type of "invisible work" and how families did this work. Members of the medical and educational communities, which both stressed oral education, further reinforced this work of deaf education in families. Many of these parents incorporated working with the deaf or deaf education as part of their own formal or informal careers, which as these stories show, was work primarily done by women.

The women in this study, some at very young ages and others later in life, also became key decision makers in their own educational processes. Their abilities to self-advocate, to be lifetime educators where they educated hearing people about their deafness, and, as one woman said, to "cope" with their deafness in all hearing educational environments affected their educational opportunities. These learned skills became tools that the women took with them as they negotiated their way in their educational settings and families. How and when the women developed these skills also shaped how they thought of themselves as deaf women.

The women, due to being pushed toward oralism and then experiencing cultural shifts later in life, as they became more integrated into Deaf culture, were in better positions to make decisions about themselves. Another finding of this study is that all of the women faced challenges regarding communication in their family and educational settings which led to each of the women struggling to find a sense of place. This struggle for place became a struggle for the women's own individual identities. Finally, each of the women fought to have equal access to education so that they might also have more options regarding their future career opportunities. In this way, the schools that these women attended became sites where they fought to obtain access to equal opportunities. Although the total number of deaf women who attend college nationally is not known, these women represent a small, yet important, group of women within the Deaf community.

DISCOVERING OR ACKNOWLEDGING DEAFNESS

All of the women in this study were thought to have been born deaf except Teresa who developed a progressive hearing loss around the age of three. Families discovered their daughter's deafness between the ages of seven months to three years old. Many of the women, including Stephanie and Ellen, who had an older deaf sibling, were taken to those who were considered "experts" who medically "diagnosed" their deafness and made recommendations to their parents for their schooling.

Reactions to Daughter's Deafness: Taking their Daughters to "Experts"

All of the parents took their daughters to "experts" to discover if they were indeed deaf. These experts included adult members of the Deaf community, hospitals, and manual and oral state residential schools for the deaf. For example, both Beth and Teresa's parents took them to members of the Deaf community to seek advice about their daughters. This often then led to a trip to a hospital or a school for the deaf where the girls underwent audio-logical tests. Beth, Teresa, and Carol were all taken to such places. Other families, such as Heather and Debbie's parents, took them to a new pre-school for the deaf, which was housed within a hearing college in Boston. Taking their daughters to "experts" happened from as early to seven months to three years old. All of these "experts" advised the parents to communicate orally with their daughters, which would later influence their educational opportunities.

Hearing Parents Teaching Oralism

Beth actually began her story with how her deafness was discovered, men-tioning that her mother suspected she was deaf before the age of two. The doctors, who in her opinion, "ignored the intuition of mothers," told her mother that everything was fine. Her parents, however, were both still wor-ried and so they took Beth to see a deaf couple who lived nearby. This cou-ple advised them to take Beth to the nearby manual state residential school for the deaf and have her undergo an audiological test:

> B: I remember walking in with my mother and my father and we went into the school office and there was a man. I didn't understand what was going on. They put me in this audiological room. How they do tested me was really strange. The reason why was because I had no communicative language yet at two. How was he going to ask me any questions? So, what he would do, he would pinch me and I would jump and he'd sign "hurt." When he pinched again and he'd sign "hurt." And I went (She flinches.). So, I went "o.k." That's when I began to understand the sign "hurt" and then he would tickle me and then I would jump and laugh and then he'd tickle me in another part and I wasn't sure if he tickled me and it's like, fun and then he'd tickle me and then pinch me, and I went, "Oh, hurt." And he'd tickle me and I went, "Oh, o.k." This is "hurt" and when he tickled me, it was tick-ling, o.k. I began to understand and that's how he sort of tested me. He put the earphones on me and I could hear something and he'd say, "hurt." And I'd go, "mmm." I was trying to figure out hurt, tickle, what, you know, try to figure out between the two. I said, "oh, tickle, o.k." That's how he evaluated my hearing.

Most of the women described going through such tests when they were young and how parents had to persist in getting their daughters "diag-nosed." Beth describes her parents as "thrilled" to find out that she was deaf:

B: The audiologist was stunned that they were happy. My father and mother said "yes, it's been a long time trying to figure out. We knew there was something there that she had to be deaf and doctors kept telling us no, and now you're confirming she's deaf, and we're thrilled." "Now, we know that she's deaf." And the audiologist said "don't teach her sign language, teach her to be oral."

In this story, Beth relates a kind of family story for both her and her family where her parents have become part of how she has come to know and remember about her deafness and early experiences. The pressure for parents to communicate orally with their children was not unique to those women who had hearing parents. As Baynton (1997) describes, in the late nineteenth century, American educators along with Alexander Graham Bell promoted oralism as the most appropriate way to educate deaf children. Thus, in the context of a larger hearing society, the women of this study grew up in a time where oralism was seen as the "norm" in both their family and early educational settings.

Deaf Parents Teaching Oralism

Janice is the only woman in this study who comes from an all deaf family, including her paternal grandparents, and considers ASL her "first language." Her all deaf family used ASL, but they also used English word order in addition to "mouth movements," which shows how even in this all deaf family there was a stress on oralism. Janice describes how her mother, who immigrated to America from Germany when she was eleven, and her father felt about her deafness as well as their own and how, at an early age, she was encouraged to speak orally and not sign:

J: Back then my parents, ashamed (She shakes her head "no" like this isn't quite the right word.) When we went public subway, signing. My mother would say, "no sign" (She makes a movement like she is her mother and puts her hands under the table with a scared look on her face.). They did not want people to look at us. No sign. Oppressed. When we went to visit our family, hearing relatives. My mother would say "talk with your voice." (She makes a motion with her hand at her throat like her voice is stuck.) Often my uncles, grandmother, and grandfather could not understand me. I would refuse to talk. I hated going to visit my mother's family. They were hearing. They couldn't understand me. Back then, my parents didn't sign. Deaf people who did not have good English were not smart. Now, they think differently, but back then listen and if not good, English, not smart.

The "benefits" of oral communication were not only reinforced by various schools and the medical community, but they were also stressed within family groups. Being brought up oral had consequences for these women's self acceptance and educational opportunities. For most women, being brought up oral led them to delay accepting their identity as a Deaf woman as well as miss critical information and to feel socially on the margins in their mainstreamed classrooms. Debbie felt that growing up oral had given her "the edge" so that she could better work in a hearing society; however, she also struggled throughout her life to ensure she had equal access to hearing classrooms.

Not all families, however, heeded the advice of the "experts" described above. In two cases, having an older deaf sibling or relative who was brought up oral, prompted families to seek other options, such as sign language, "total communication" methods, or sending their daughters to manual state residential schools for the deaf.

Family Experiences

All of the women discussed being in between worlds in their families while growing up and learning how to communicate within their family groups. How they learned ASL and English influenced their relationships with family members and how the women thought of themselves. The family, then, became a place where these women continually did the work of going back and forth between two worlds and developed their identities as Deaf women.

Nine of the ten women came from families with hearing parents. Of these nine families, three have siblings who were deaf. Stephanie and Ellen have an older deaf sibling whereas Heather's deaf sibling is younger. Janice, the only woman in this study to come from an all deaf family, has an older deaf brother. Two of the six women who grew up in all hearing families and two of the three women who had hearing parents and a deaf sibling described often feeling left out of their family groups in various situations and family events. Although this continues today, they and the members of their families continue to do the work of going back and forth between these worlds. As with any family, rituals such as attending family gatherings were places where they developed their definitions of family. The rituals of family time activities were embedded in the larger social context of a hearing society. Communication and language became key aspects of how these families developed and how the women began to think of themselves as deaf, hearing, or in between.

All Hearing Families

After learning sign through interacting with people in the Deaf community and later attending NTID where she learned ASL, Carol would communicate in oral English when at home with her family:

Carol: I learned sign really fast from deaf social. Some of them knew sign, so I picked it up from them. But not really sign because I'm always around with hearing people. I don't really use it that much. But, when I was in college, I used it every day because all of my friends signed and everything. I get frustrated when my family's sitting and having dinner. They talk. "What are you guys talking about?" "Oh never mind. I'll tell you later." Or they tell me brief. "Oh, you guys said more than that." I hate going to my cousin's house. (She signs, "I'm the only one, boring.") My brother's been good. He'll sit next to me and he'll tell me. But, he's bored too. Brother, sister same.

While learning ASL in college, Carol came home and was also learning how to negotiate being in between the hearing and Deaf worlds in her family. Her story shows the sense of isolation she felt in her all hearing family and how her brother helped her to negotiate her identity. Through her educational and family experiences, Carol began developing strategies for negotiating between these worlds. She did this by continually asking her hearing family to translate for her and by learning ASL to communicate with members of the Deaf community. These experiences helped to shape how she has come to see herself as a deaf woman.

Marie, who also felt left out of her all hearing family, suggests the invisible work involved in family events:

M: There are times even today that I feel left out of the family's conversation. I know that family are aware and they are trying their best to include me. But it is not a natural thing.

By describing this work as not "natural," Marie suggests that trying to ensure communication between these two worlds in one's hearing family is a learned skill. The work which these families do in an effort to develop family relationships shapes how these women see themselves as deaf and also shapes their ideas about being in the hearing world.

Families with Another Deaf Sibling

With the exception of Janice, who came from an all deaf family, the three women who had another deaf sibling in their hearing family experiences were slightly different from the women who came from all hearing families. Birth order also played a role in these relationships. Ellen learned ASL from her older deaf brother at a slightly younger age than the women from all hearing families:

E: I learned sign when I was eight. Through my brother. At the other school, he learned sign. I liked it better. Sign.

C: And you prefer ASL?

E: Yes.

With the exception of Beth, who attended a manual state residential school for the deaf and whose mother taught her sign, Ellen learned her native language of ASL at an earlier age than the six women from all hearing families. She developed a strong Deaf identity at a younger age than most of these women and is currently raising her two deaf daughters to be proud of their Deaf identity and use ASL as their native language. Her early family experiences and learning ASL from her older deaf brother influenced how she thinks of herself and her children as deaf.

Heather and her younger deaf brother became close because of this similar experience of being between worlds and growing up in a strong oral environment:

H: When we were small we weren't that close. I was three years older than him. But as we got older we were very close. And our hearing brother had his own friends. But my deaf brother and I stayed home a lot. I was lucky to have a deaf brother because the rest of my family is hearing. I would see them laugh or I would see them and I would say "what are you talking about"? And they'd say "oh, nothing, nothing important." It was common for them to say that. Sometimes I feel left out, but I have a deaf brother, so we're very close. Today, I get together with my family, it's still the same story. Sometimes they will slow down for me. But it's easy to forget.

Having a deaf sibling helped Heather not feel as isolated in her otherwise all hearing family. Since she was older, however, she would later teach her deaf brother sign, which she learned at NTID. She also mentioned that she developed more of a social life when attending NTID and interacting with people from the Deaf community. Since she and her deaf brother stayed at home most weekends in high school, she did not develop many social networks until she learned ASL and accepted herself as deaf. The experiences, then, of women who came from families with deaf siblings differed somewhat from those women who came from all hearing families. They also differed in ways *among* these family groups such as having an older or younger deaf sibling.

Women's Acknowledging their own Deafness

All of the women spoke of when they acknowledged their own deafness for the first time. Although this occurred at varying stages in their lives, one common experience was when the women first began learning ASL and were exposed to the Deaf community or another group of individuals who were constructed as "disabled," which affected how they thought of themselves as deaf. This experience also fostered a sense of belonging to the Deaf community and eventually led to acceptance of oneself as deaf. The most common story was experiencing "culture shock" when first being integrated into the Deaf community and exposed to Deaf culture, often upon entering NTID, RIT, Gallaudet or a manual state residential school for the deaf. This experience was linked to the women "picking up" sign language in various forms and integrating themselves socially with the Deaf community.

Belonging in the Deaf World

Both Kristen and Heather started at hearing colleges, and then made the decision to transfer to RIT. Prior to transferring, their stories also include descriptions of the extensive extra work that they did to ensure their academic success, such as staying up late, asking friends to take notes and then double checking with their professors that the notes were accurate, and reading their textbooks several times. Heather's visit with a deaf friend at NTID the summer after her first year at her hearing college was a critical turning point in her life:

> H: I think it was a good decision for me in my life. Because for the first time, I experienced seeing so many deaf people. And I'm dying to take a class at NTID, at RIT. It was my first time in an all deaf class. I was used to all hearing. At the same time, learning sign language. That summer was the first time that I identified myself as a deaf person. Before, I hated being deaf. I wished I was hearing. It's an awful feeling. Awful. But, when I was around deaf people, I really can communicate. Not like the hearing world. I could communicate, but only one on one, not in group of people. Now with a group of deaf people, I can understand. Sign is very easy to learn. That summer, I was nineteen.

Although she identified herself to me as deaf, not Deaf, Heather, as with all of the other women, had a sense of belonging to the Deaf community. This had an effect on her learning experiences in college and connects with when she began "picking up" ASL. As with Kristen, both of these women described how transferring to RIT helped to improve their grades, which influenced their self esteem as young deaf women.

A major turning point for Teresa occurred in the summer after her freshman year at a hearing college when she worked at a church conference center in the South with a staff of four hundred other students, three of whom were also deaf. Unlike Teresa, however, these deaf students were all "manualists." As part of this experience, she participated in a church choir and experienced signing in public for the first time. At home in her father's church in the Midwest, her parents had helped to create a deaf community, mostly of manualists, within their church. But Teresa, because of her oralist upbringing, had not been able to communicate with them. She recalls how she was excited that she had learned sign language and would be able to go home and communicate with the deaf members of her church:

> T: What really helped was the last week of the summer conference they would get everyone to get up to sing in a church choir in the auditorium on that final night. They called the four of us to come up and sign too. So, I had to learn from them. "Our Father, who art in Heaven." The Lord's Prayer, that was my first length because I had to memorize. In public. (She lifts her hands up and out as if to command an audience.) I was excited because (She makes the sign for "same.") You know that age, same. (She smiles). I came home, I saw the people in church, I said, "Hi, our Father, who art in Heaven, hallowed be thy name." (laughing). "I learned sign." Then, someone said, "why don't you go to Gallaudet?" I never heard of Gallaudet. (She signs "deaf college" and whispers it.). Before that I don't know sign. I'm not interested. I think I'm one of the few who said (She signs "sign for who? I'm not interested."). Because most people (She signs "let's get together you are deaf" excitedly). But, me, I stayed at my college in [the South] and graduated in four years. And I worked each summer at the center. I met more deaf people, but still, I preferred to stay the way I was. Comfort zone, I guess. Going to Washington, D.C. I don't think my parents would have let me go anyway. (She shakes her head "no" vigorously). World out there. So, that was my introduction into the deaf world. I guess today I'm in the other deaf world.

Learning sign language for the first time helped Teresa have a sense of belonging where she felt like she was the "same" as other members of the Deaf community. Despite this, she articulates how she felt a part of the Deaf community and yet also did not feel totally part of this group due to her oral education. Like all of these women, she was learning the art of "going back and forth" between the worlds of the deaf and the hearing. Teresa describes the differences *within* the Deaf community and how being an oralist, manualist, or a combination of both shapes one's life experiences. Her sense of herself as a deaf woman has changed over time as Teresa now considers herself in the "other deaf world" where she lives in Rochester.

Feeling like an "Oral Failure"

Stephanie experienced her sense of belonging with other deaf individuals while also feeling like she did not belong in her oral mainstreamed classroom. Despite her teacher's encouragement, she felt like an "oral failure" because she was not able to speak English like her hearing classmates. Her older deaf sister was in the same school, but in a different class where each "special class" consisted of ten deaf children. She describes her experiences at the public school and how it impacted her identity with the Deaf community:

> S: The teacher would say "oh, you talk good."(She pretends she's a teacher talking to a student.) I knew I wasn't because when I would go out on the street or in another class, the kids couldn't understand me. My deaf friends in my class, we knew who talked better. Teacher thought she was smarter than me. I've always been good staying with my deaf group because I feel like I belong. Outside we would see each other for lunch, recess. After school wait for the school bus. That was good enough. Did not have many hearing friends. Experience of talking to the teacher, I kind of got tired of trying to speech. I feel like it's a waste of my time. I knew I was not speaking like hearing people. I just want to study English, History, but had to stop, speech. That was a negative experience. But a positive experience. I was not alone. Go around with all of my [deaf] friends.

Stephanie speaks to the pros and cons of being in an oral environment early on in her educational experience. Her story points to a certain hierarchy within the deaf students at the public hearing school with those that could "do talking" in the hegemonic way at the top and others who struggled with English seen, in this context, as deficient. Feeling like an "oral failure" is, of course, also based on the context of her being mainstreamed into a hearing classroom. The "negatives" of this experience were that she wanted to learn the material, such as English and History, but had to take time out for speech lessons. The "positives," which she created for herself in the mainstreamed environment, were that she was able to connect socially with a group, other children who were deaf, and feel like she belonged.

This experience had major consequences for Stephanie's educational opportunities. Because of this experience, she told her parents that she wanted to attend a manual state residential school for the deaf and did so for junior high and high school where, as she describes, her "mind was open" and she began feeling not only socially connected to the Deaf community, but was also academically successful. This led Stephanie to attend Gallaudet University, travel abroad, and work with the Indian Deaf community as a Regional Interpreter and Translator. She would seek employment at a manual state residential school for the deaf where she continues to work with the Deaf community as an ASL Specialist. She lives in Rochester where there is a large Deaf community. The experiences of feeling a sense of belonging to the Deaf community at an early age, and conversely, a sense of not belonging to the hearing world, influenced not only the type of work that she does, but the fact that she lives and works in the deaf world.

"Accepting" Oneself as Deaf

Kristen's experience of connecting with a group of people with cerebral palsy and accepting herself as "different" is another example of how some of these women accepted or acknowledged their deafness. Her first job experience in high school was working with children who had CP, which made her think about her own career goals:

> K: I still worked there as a volunteer because at that time, I was still thinking I'm different than other people. Why do I always have to work so hard? What about me? Why can't I have everything? I talk to my parents about that. They said "you need to meet other special people." So, I went to work there and that's when I realized it's not worth feeling sorry for myself. Stop. Accept. Move forward. That's what I enjoy, working with people.

Kristen, by working with other children who were considered "different," began to "accept" herself as a deaf woman. She comments that "at that time," she thought of herself as different, which suggests that her thinking has shifted and that she might not see herself as all that different now, despite the fact that she identifies herself as a Deaf woman.

Kristen transferred from her hearing college to NTID because she could both communicate and socially integrate herself with the Deaf community within a larger hearing college. This connects with her earlier experience of accepting herself as being part of both worlds:

> K: I was able to take more classes. I was able to get involved in more social. I don't have to do midnight until three in the morning no more. It was great. Best of both worlds here. Here you have hearing classmates and deaf friends. And I know that with my deafness, I need to

take on the highest education that is possible so that I can work in the
hearing society.

Despite her desire to work in the "hearing society," Kristen is happy in her
current position where she now works at NTID. She discusses how, in a context such as RIT and NTID where she had the social support of the larger
Deaf community, she was able to succeed academically. Her story also suggests how critical becoming bilingual is for these women in terms of their educational opportunities. Kristen's descriptions of "hearing classmates" and
"deaf friends" show that while she was integrated with hearing students in the
classroom and had the support of interpreters, she still considered her friends
to be people who were part of the Deaf community. Her story is an example
of how schools were places where the women learned how to negotiate being
in between worlds not only socially, but also academically. All of the women
would use this learned skill to continually negotiate places for themselves.

"Culture Shock" at a Deaf College

Six of the deaf women spoke of experiencing "culture shock" when they
entered a deaf college for the first time. Although she attended and lived at
an oral state residential school for the deaf and grew up in an all deaf family, Janice describes this "cultural shock" when she attended Gallaudet:

> J: When I went to Gallaudet, (She gives a look of surprise.) cultural
>   shock. Even though I was from a deaf family. But, in the classes,
>   signing, (She raises her hand and then makes a sign that looks like
>   "communication.").
>
> C: You're trying to lip read.
>
> J: Right. Frustrating. School. (She gives a look of shock.)

Janice links the type of "culture shock" that she experienced to learning the
new language of "signing," specifically ASL, in her classes. This shift in her
education also had a positive influence on Janice, as she began to raise her
hand and talk more in her classes and became more socially outgoing as she
was integrated into the Deaf community. After an adjustment period, which
included learning ASL and acceptance of oneself as deaf, this culture shock
or shift often led these women to make places for themselves, as Janice did,
in the deaf world.

"Picking up" American Sign Language

As the women began acknowledging their own deafness, all of them had the
experience of "picking up" ASL. They did so both in formal classrooms, by

watching the interpreters, and in various social settings, such as at Deaf clubs or in the dorms. Kristen describes learning ASL, in a more covert way, at her oral school where sign language was forbidden:

> K: I lived in the dorm Monday through Friday and come home on the weekends. For five years. I was two and half until eight years old. During that five years, I learned ASL. In the dorm and in the playground. And deaf family would sleep over and I would meet deaf adults. Signing. Just pick it up, naturally. But, I talked orally in the classroom and at home. I never signed at home.

As with many of these women, Kristen had specific places, such as at home with her all hearing family and in the classroom, where she specifically did not use sign language. Her description of learning ASL by "naturally" picking it up in social settings with other deaf adults suggests that, in addition to her years of oral education, she considers ASL to be one of her primary languages and herself a part of the Deaf community. Learning ASL was a critical piece in identifying herself as a Deaf woman because she felt a sense of belonging to the Deaf community.

PARENTS' DECISIONS ABOUT EDUCATION

After parents discovered that their daughters were deaf, they had major decisions to make about their education. As mentioned earlier, all were encouraged to educate their daughters orally. The experiences of a family who had exposure to the Deaf community or a deaf relative in their family differed in some ways from those parents who had no knowledge of the Deaf community. Also related to this experience was whether the parents themselves were hearing or deaf. These factors influenced the women's educational opportunities and how they navigated their identities as deaf women.

Family's Resistance to "Expert" Advice

Resistance to Oralism in Families with Hearing Parents

All but one of the women's families were strong supporters of oral education, as they were told by "experts" that it would later create better educational opportunities for their daughters. Having a relative who was deaf or being exposed to the Deaf community in some ways led three of the families into knowing some of the drawbacks of an oral education and some of the benefits of learning sign language. Beth, whose mother had a cousin who was deaf, describes her mother's reaction to the audiologist at the oral state residential school for the deaf when he told her to teach her daughter to be oral:

> B: My mother went, "oh forget that," because she had a distant cousin who was deaf. My mother went "no, I've already watched my cousin grow up signing" and she just dismissed his attitude towards sign language. And they went to the store and bought a book on sign language and they brought it home. She went to the deaf school and told them that she wanted to put me into a kindergarten program so that I could associate with other deaf kids and deaf people. I was between the ages of two to five. I mingled with the kids there and when it came time for me to attend school I went into the School for the Deaf. The school was a manual school. There was a really a strong ASL program and some of the teachers I had to use simple oral methods 'cause some of the teachers refused to learn sign. I could kind of go back and forth.

Beth's experience was unusual; however, all parents at some point in their daughter's educational lives began to incorporate both manual and oral methods. Nine of the families sent their daughter to an oral school, but incorporated sign language at home by using "home signs" or signs which only the family used. This sign language was not ASL, which would allow the girls to identify with the Deaf community and Deaf culture, yet it often created a bridge for when they would learn ASL later in life. One consequence of teaching some form of sign language at home was that it privatized deaf education into the home while schools were focusing on mainstreaming deaf students and using oral methods. All of the girls were continually negotiating using ASL, SEE, and spoken English in various settings and still do today. This often shaped their identities and acceptance of themselves as deaf women. Beth's example is illustrative of this "going back and forth" between these languages and methods of communication. Despite Beth being at a manual school, many teachers refused to learn sign language of any kind and so she learned at an early age to adjust her communication style and language in various settings.

Sometimes, it was the daughter who told her parents that she wanted to learn sign language or to attend a manual state residential school for the deaf and then the parents would support their daughter's decision. In two cases where the daughter had an older sibling who was deaf, such as Stephanie and Ellen, there was usually more support for this choice. Stephanie's story illustrates this finding. After being mainstreamed in her public elementary school with her older deaf sister, she described to me how she wanted to go to the manual state school for the deaf and how her mother, perhaps because of seeing Stephanie's older sister struggle with being mainstreamed, later agreed to send her to the manual state residential school for the deaf:

> S: That fall I was supposed to go [to the public junior high school] with some deaf kids. I remember what my deaf sister told me that she struggled in junior high school. In junior high school they had day class. That's good, but they wanted to go to each class with the hearing. Mainstream. My sister told me about her experience. I had a fieldtrip and I understand how hard it is for my sister. That made me not want to go to that school. And mother let me go [to the manual state residential school for the deaf]. I think maybe my mother not like me go away, but she understood.

Having seen her older deaf sister struggle in public school as well as experiencing it herself, Stephanie was able to advocate for herself to her parents that she wanted to attend the manual state residential school for the deaf. With her mother's assistance, she was able to attend this school for her junior high and high school. Her mother also helped Stephanie take a sign language class in the community before she entered this school so that she would have a smoother transition to a manual environment.

Having an older deaf sibling helped Stephanie and her parents to negotiate her education in ways they did not for her sister. This shows the incredible responsibility placed on the parents to know how to best educate their daughters. Stephanie, who went to the manual state residential school for the deaf and then on to Gallaudet, accepted herself as a Deaf woman at an earlier age than most. She was the only person in her family to attend college, including her parents, who both had an eighth grade education and worked as farmers. The decision to attend the manual state residential school for the deaf increased Stephanie's educational opportunities by networking her into a school where people would later attend college.

Resistance to Manualism in a Family with Deaf Parents

Unlike Beth and Stephanie's parents, Janice's deaf parents wanted Janice and her older deaf brother to attend an oral state residential school for the deaf because, being deaf themselves, they saw how manualism could put them at a disadvantage in a hearing world. Her parents resisted the perspective of the larger Deaf community which supported learning ASL. Janice tells how they made the decision to send her and her older brother to the oral school:

> J: My parents were struggling. We lived in [a northeastern state].
> They didn't want me to go to [the state] School for the Deaf. They
> wanted me to go to the [another state] School for the deaf. The
> School for the Deaf [where we lived] was not oral. My [deaf] grand-
> mother went to the [the oral deaf] school. My parents wanted oral
> training for me. My parents decided to take me there and sleep there
> at the school. I was maybe one or two. My parents moved to be near
> the city. For my brother school. That was the only school I went to.
> Oral. No sign language. Permanent school. Fine. (She looks off to the
> side smiling, then frowns, and gives a look like "not really fine.")
> (long pause).

Although Janice's parents decided to educate her at an oral state residential
school for the deaf, they did this as an act of resistance to "experts" in the
Deaf community, much like Beth and Stephanie's parents, to give their
daughter what they saw as the best educational opportunity. Although Janice felt socially connected to her peers in school, when she later attended
Gallaudet, was exposed to the Deaf community, and learned ASL, she went
through an identity shift.

Stephanie and Beth, whose hearing parents were influenced by older
deaf relatives to send their daughters to manual schools and Janice's parents, in part because of being deaf themselves, wanted Janice and her older
brother to be schooled orally suggests that having deaf or hearing parents
along with an older deaf relative influenced these families' decisions about
their daughters' educations. The families of these women, then, also
became part of the story of decisions about the women's educations. This
would later shape the women's educational opportunities and how they
thought of themselves as deaf.

Parents Became Teachers for their Daughters at Home

The Invisible Work of Teaching

Six women told me about experiences in their homes where their parents or
relatives either formally or informally acted as providers of deaf education
for their daughters. This sometimes meant private formal speech lessons, as
with Janice and her older deaf brother and Marie or taking their daughters
to sign language classes in the community, as with Stephanie and her older
deaf sister and Carol or having a relative who was a doctor and could test
her hearing and teach her to use her residual hearing, as with Teresa. Or it
might refer to informal lessons, such as those Beth described her mother
giving her when she was two years old:

B: They were showing me the sign language book and I remember the first picture was an apple. And my mother pointed at the apple and she signed "apple" and I was not really quite understanding. So my mother went to the refrigerator, got an actual apple and pointed to it and said, "apple" and then pointed to the picture. I looked at the picture and the actual apple and her signing apple and I went, "oh." I made the connection between the two. From that point, my vocabulary just grew, particularly through the use of that book with my mother.

Beth's example highlights the invisible and often visible work that these parents, particularly the mothers, were doing with their young daughters to communicate with them. Various authors have chronicled the gendered nature of invisible work of mothers who have children with "disabilities" (Harris, 2003; Traustadottir, 1992). In three cases, the parents of these women became involved in deaf education, deaf ministry, and advocacy. Carol and Debbie's mothers, who were both trained as teachers, appear to incorporate this work into their lives more easily by becoming teachers of the deaf. Debbie's father also became involved with deaf education by being on the board of the oral state residential school for the deaf which she attended. Teresa's father, a minister of a church, and mother who was principal of the church's Vacation Bible School, incorporated this work by including the Deaf community in their ministry efforts. These actions were part of parents' strategies of becoming involved in deaf education to ensure better opportunities for their daughters and shaped the lives of their families.

The Role of Gender: "She was like a teacher"

Kristen, whose father worked as a chemical engineer and who went to various private, religious, hearing schools, also mentioned to me that her mother worked with her at home on her education:

K: She met my father and when they got married, she didn't have to work. So, she spent a lot of time working with me. She was like a teacher, full-time with me. She's very supportive of education. Reading, writing, involved in people.

Much like Beth's mother, Kristen describes how her mother worked with her on her education in the home. Of the six cases where women mentioned that their relatives were informal providers of deaf education in the home, five of the women mentioned that it was their mothers who fulfilled this role in their family while one, in Teresa's case, was a grandfather. This role in these families, then, is gendered with the mothers of these women doing the majority of the work.

Another example of where gender plays a role in these at home educations is in Ellen's story. Ellen, who grew up oral, and her family, especially her father, rarely used sign language at home. They did use some "home signs" as other families have described. Ellen mentioned that her other three brothers "sign a little bit," her sister is " a very good signer" and would often interpret for her, and her mother is "pretty good," "but my father's not." She also mentioned, and eight of the other women in this story confirm, that hearing parents and siblings not being fluent in ASL is a "normal" experience. She recalls how her father, who ran his own locksmith business, found it challenging to learn sign language. She states, "My father worked seven days. Long time ago. Work, work, work, so much. Sign. Not have time."

Ellen's description here of her father not having enough time to learn sign language due to his work schedule shows how larger ideas about gender roles affect these at home educations. Although unlike Kristen's mother, Ellen's mother worked full-time, she was still seen as the parent who knew sign language. Since deaf education was partly privatized in the home, gender played a greater role than social class in these family's experiences. These types of experiences would later influence the deaf women's educational opportunities. Ellen, after working for five years after high school, would later struggle to put herself through college. Unfortunately, she was not able to complete her degree; however, she has hopes of returning to finish.

Teaching Families

Seven women told me stories of how their siblings also became part of this at home teaching experience. Ellen's older brother, who went to an oral state residential school for the deaf, taught her sign language at home when she was eight. In all of the three cases where women had a deaf sibling in an all hearing family, the women formed a close bond with their deaf sibling that remains in place today. There were also times when hearing siblings were involved in teaching the deaf women, such as in Debbie's case, where her younger brother and sister would teach her things by writing on a blackboard that they had in their home:

> D: I'm the oldest. In a way, I had to set things up. My sister and brother relish their moments teaching me. There's a lot of concepts because I was delayed in reading, delaying in writing because I couldn't hear. They knew already. They would (She pretends to write on the blackboard.) write on the blackboard. "oh, this word means." They would

teach me. They would "oh, I'm teaching my older sister, this, this, this." (She counts off on one hand.) That was important to them. If I was a baby, the situation would have been a lot different.

As the oldest, Debbie saw herself as having to "set things up" for her younger brother and sister. She considered herself a role model to them and yet there were also times when they taught her various things related to English. These kinds of experiences and work done by families served to further privatize deaf education in the family as well as affect how these women learned language and thought of themselves as deaf.

In one case, a hearing sibling teaching English worked in ways that was sometimes not as helpful, as described by Marie, whose older hearing brother made her speak a certain way:

> M: I'm one of seven and they're all hearing. Sometimes I feel left out. Sometimes I ask my mother,"what you talking about?" She'll say, "wait a minute, let me tell you after I finish." Then, I say "o.k." Then, after you finish, "what are you saying?" "Oh, I forget." Or a very simple thing. Not (She puts her hands out as if to say "elaborate.") One good story. But they're very good to me. They try to help me. They try to get me involved. One of my brothers is very strict with me. He tries pushing me down, or you should talk like that. He tries to make me say some words the right way. I get frustrated. Like (She points outside.) snow. Ssssnnnow! I'm like (She puts her hands up in the air as if to say "oh well."). But, overall they were good. They support me. When I married John. He is one of ten. And they were making sure I was included in all of their conversations. Big difference from my family. I was kind of jealous. He has another who is deaf also. There are two of them.

Having two deaf siblings in her husband's all hearing family made this family seem more inclusive to Marie than her own family. The three deaf women in this study who had hearing parents and another deaf sibling, however, did not describe their families as necessarily being more inclusive than those who did not have another deaf sibling. Having a deaf sibling in an all hearing family helped with feelings of isolation, but did not play a role in whether the hearing members of these families learned ASL. Feeling left out at home would later shape Marie's wish to attend public school so that she could be like her hearing brothers and sisters. She, in part because of her family experience, then, is more a part of the hearing world. This experience also influenced her decision to attend RIT where she had the benefit of a Deaf community along with a hearing college experience.

As suggested in Debbie's story, the teaching in these families also comes from the deaf women themselves. All of them spoke of teaching their families sign language or about Deaf culture. One example is Beth's story of how she taught her family ASL. Early in her life, she had asked her family to stop signing to her and speak so that she could "improve" her English skills. Later, she would change her mind about this decision; however, this experience led her to discover how she was actually teaching them her native language, ASL:

> B: When I first met my husband, we went to meet my family. He said, "your family is really good at speaking ASL. They don't speak English." And I said, "no they're speaking English." He goes, "no, they are speaking ASL. They're using words but they're putting in ASL grammatic order for you. When they speak to other people they speak English. When they speak to you, they're speaking ASL. When they're sitting around the dinner table and everything they were really speaking ASL." So I asked my mother, "Are you speaking to me in ASL?" And she went, "Well yeah." And I went, "Why?" My mother said, "If I'd spoken English you'd never understood me. So when I put in ASL order, you understood me."

> C: How did they learn ASL?

> B: They learned from communicating with me. I was learning, I'd go home and I just be using ASL. I was just being myself and my brother and sister would be like watching me and they'd follow me and you know we'd just functioned as a family. My mother had very good receptive skills and understood me. 'Cause she really tried to use the facial expressions or the grammatical structures if she could but she really wasn't really proficient at. My brother and sister picked right up on it, and we've always had our own communication style.

Due to Beth's informal teaching and just being herself, her family "picked right up" on learning ASL. The women, like Beth, who used ASL at home during an early stage in their lives were extremely skillful at "going back and forth." By negotiating a place for herself in her early family experiences, Beth now has a strong Deaf identity, lives in Rochester, and works at NTID.

Parents' Strategies of Becoming Involved in Deaf Education

Another area where parents made critical decisions about their daughter's educations was in their own careers, specifically in deaf education, deaf ministry, and advocacy. Through these venues, the work of parents became more "visible" as this oftentimes included paid positions. Various researchers have documented how mothers of children with disabilities sometimes make careers out of raising their children (Harris, 2003; Traustadottir, 1992). This study shows that the experiences were similar for these deaf women's parents; however, the roles of manualism and oralism were critical ones to these experiences.

It's All in the Family

In two cases, the girls' parents were already working in educational fields and when they found out their daughter was deaf, they went specifically into deaf education. Carol's mother, a teacher by training, became a teacher of the deaf and the Director of an oral state residential school for the deaf that Carol later attended. Debbie's father was on the School Board of the oral state residential school for the deaf that she attended and her mother, a public school teacher by training, became a teacher of the deaf and a trustee of the small, private, hearing school which Debbie attended for junior high. Her parents were also involved in volunteer work, which Debbie now does as a member of a social service agency in Boston, which provides services and legal advice for members of the deaf community. While Debbie was in school, her parents were constantly "in close contact" with her teachers and were in on the decision making for her education. In both of these families, the parents wanted their daughters educated orally, but also worked to include sign language in their educations.

Debbie shows how her mother played a role in her decision to attend a hearing college instead of NTID. She said, "My mother said, 'you won't be happy [at NTID]. You will be happy socially, but the homework, you won't be happy with it.'" Due to her parents' occupations and advice, Debbie attended a hearing college with the understanding that she would be challenged, which would lead to more job opportunities. While Debbie also was part of this decision making process, her parents had a major influence on her decision. She also mentioned how she saw her older classmates from the oral state residential school for the deaf attend NTID and struggle in the workforce. As one of the younger women in this study, the privilege of her generation, in some ways, allowed her to see which would give her the most educational opportunities. Still, she was constantly doing the work of self-advocacy and educating her teachers and peers about her needs in her educational settings.

Deaf Education and Communities

Teresa's parents, much like Carol and Debbie's, incorporated deafness into their ministry associated with her father's church. Teresa's first job experience was working as a "teacher" in this church, teaching Bible lessons to deaf children in their summer time Vacation Bible School. Her mother, who was also the principal of this school, had the idea to involve Teresa:

T: They had a little boy. He was something like eight years old. His mother volunteered to help Vacation Bible School. She had to bring her boy to the school. He was deaf. I had been going to VBS all my life every summer with the hearing kids (She makes a noise and motions her hand in a circle as if to say that she was integrated with them.). That summer I was a little bit too old, getting bored. The mother didn't know what to do with her boy. He was (She makes a sign like someone is running around.). My mother said, "Teresa will watch him." She came up with the idea to have a class for deaf children. She said "Teresa, why don't you teach them what you have learned from VBS all your life?" So, I taught my first class for deaf children. This was all oral. We got into the newspaper. I have a picture of me holding up a pencil because a photographer came. (She grabs a piece of paper.). And he said, "now, Teresa, you be signing to them." I go (She gives a look like "what?"). We don't sign. So he says "well, do something." So, I (She holds up the paper and points the pencil to it while mouthing pretend words.) So, you see me there with a book (She holds the paper up and gives a posed smile.).

Teresa's parents hired a certified interpreter for the church and eventually the deaf membership of the congregation grew to about thirty people. However, Teresa's description of her teaching at the VBS indicates that the school remained oral, which influenced how she saw herself as a deaf woman. Teresa attended a hearing college and did not identify with the Deaf community until much later in her life when she moved to Rochester with her husband and children. Her early teaching experiences would lead Teresa to teach at NTID where she used ASL in the classroom. Similar to many of these deaf women's experiences, she was seen as a legitimate teacher in the deaf world; however, she did not work at a hearing school teaching hearing children. The fact that her father and mother used their work to connect to the Deaf community seemingly opened opportunities for her; however, these opportunities were in the Deaf world.

WOMEN'S DECISIONS ABOUT EDUCATION

While parents made decisions about their daughter's educations, the women themselves also played important roles in their own educational decision making processes. All of the women spoke to me about their role as "self-advocates" and "lifetime educators" in their educational settings, especially in all hearing schools. They talked about other strategies, which involved being outgoing, observing, and becoming involved in sports and extra curricular activities, as ways of "coping" with deafness and resisting stereotypes of having a "disability." How the women negotiated their roles was not only linked to how they saw themselves as deaf women, but also related to how they communicated at home and in their classrooms. How "well" these deaf women were able to negotiate these three roles had major consequences for their educational opportunities. One finding of this study is that, as the women made decisions about their educations, they also struggled to find their places for themselves. Lane (1999) has argued that education is the battleground where linguistic minorities, such as those in the Deaf community, win or lose their rights. The stories of these deaf women, who each consider themselves as part of this linguistic minority, show how through the process of their daily interactions they engaged in a fight for their rights as a linguistic minority. Therefore, their struggle to develop and maintain their identities as part of the Deaf community in a larger hearing society can be viewed as a political fight for their own individuality as a minority group.

Self-Advocates in their Educational Experiences

Wanting to be in the Hearing World

Six of the women spoke of several instances where they advocated for themselves to be in hearing classrooms, which shows that they were, in some ways, trying to "fit in" with the hearing world. Marie attended preschool through the sixth grade at a public high school outside of her home town because this school had a special program for the deaf. The school had four rooms of deaf children who were separate from the hearing classrooms and taught speech lessons in what she termed "special education" classes. Marie describes how she explained to her parents and her elementary school teachers that she wanted to be in the classrooms with the hearing students:

> M: When I first started at two and a half up to sixth grade, I was in that special program, deaf program, most of the time. Then, I was very, um, protest. I want to be in with the hearing people. So, my parents said "o.k." So, they put me into a hearing classroom. It started off with the math. With my higher skills. They tried me when I was in second grade. I did well in hearing classroom, but the English was in a special program. It needs to improved a lot. So, I moved out of third in math and then when I got into fourth grade, I started reading and geography in a hearing classroom. And it increased little by little. I told my parents, "I really want to go into the hearing classroom, full-time." But, my parents had to hold me back because of my English. So, I never was

in a perfect grade. I was like fifth grade math, fourth grade English, fourth grade geography. So, I would never be in all level grades. So, I got frustrated by that. I want to make me (She makes a sign that looks like "level.") normal in one level. It was frustrating. I was never really social with hearing kids that much. I'm not sure why. A lot of times, the deaf kids I hang around. I play with the hearing kids a little bit. It was more of going to the classroom. When it was time to go back, I'd go. So, I never had the opportunity to interact with the hearing.

Marie's story shows how, at a very young age, she was learning the skills of being, as she described, "self-advocate." Her "special education" program for the deaf segregated her from hearing children not only academically, but also socially. This experience and strategy that she developed of advocating for herself shaped how she would later continue to do this with her peers in college. It also played a role in how she thought of herself as a deaf woman when she went to RIT and learned ASL.

Heather's story of why she first chose to attend a hearing college instead of NTID connects with Marie's story because she too wanted to be with hearing students. Related to this was her desire to exert her own independence and make decisions for herself about her own education:

> H: Really in my head it was my first choice, but my parents told me to go to NTID. I wanted to go to NTID. But the problem was (laughs), my parents, were hoping that I would go to NTID, but I felt like it was not my decision. It was my parents' decision. I want mine. I had a strong drive to be independent because in high school, I felt I was not independent enough. I had to depend on my parents to make phone calls and make decisions for me. It was my decision to go to the [hearing college]. They told me that it was up to me, but they were hoping that I would go to NTID. But, I felt it was not my decision.
>
> C: That's so interesting and then you ended up going to NTID and RIT. (laughs)
>
> H: Yeah. But, I first [hearing college]. My decision. So, independent from my parents.

Heather's description of advocating for herself as a way of exerting her independence is another example of how these deaf women resisted being labeled as "different" and stigmatized as "disabled" in the context of an all hearing school. Heather did not want to attend NTID because she did not want to be seen as deaf and "different" from her peers. Marie and Heather, who both grew up oral, saw themselves as more in the hearing world until they began learning ASL and were exposed to the Deaf community in Rochester. Despite this, Heather stated that, in her mind, NTID and RIT was her "first choice'; however, she wanted it to be her decision. Also, her decision was influenced by her later exposure to NTID and members of the Deaf community. The experiences of identifying as a deaf woman and learning ASL had a later influence on these women's self-advocacy. These experiences would influence not only their educational opportunities, but would also influence how they thought of themselves as deaf women.

Knowing the Politics of Education

Four of the women, as Marie did, spoke of wanting to be considered "normal" in their hearing classrooms and would, as an act of resistance to being stereotyped as unintelligent, often refuse interpreters to avoid continually being marked and stigmatized as different. In this way, the women had to partially deny their needs as deaf women. Carol attended the public school system in her home town from the second grade until she graduated from high school. Like Marie, she had no interpreters or note takers at this school, but did see a "special needs" teacher daily during study hall. This woman was not a teacher of the deaf and had no training in deaf education, which suggests that the program stressed oralism. Carol, like many of these women, would ask her friend to use carbon paper so that she could get a copy of the notes. She told me why she did not have an interpreter by staying that, "Mom wanted me to have an interpreter when I was in high school, I refused. My mom said 'oh, it will be very helpful to you.' 'No,' I said, 'peer pressure.' I said, 'I'm fine.' I have a friend who sits next to me who takes notes. It was a carbon copy paper."

Carol's story shows how she worked to feel socially connected and tried not to identify herself as different by having a sign language interpreter and risk being stigmatized by her peers, despite the advice of her mother, who was a teacher for the deaf. She was able to develop some type of social connection by having a hearing friend take notes. After attending NTID, learning ASL, and having interpreters, Carol realized that it would have been easier for her to have interpreters in high school and said that she wished that she had listened to her mother's advice. Learning the skill of self-advocacy, much like the process of acknowledging one's deafness, is an ongoing process for these deaf women.

Marie's story of how she struggled to attend the high school in her home town connects with Carol's story of wanting to fit in with her hearing classmates. Like Carol and some of the other women, Marie describes how she reluctantly agreed to a teacher for the deaf so that she could attend this school:

M: When I was in junior high school, I heard that in [my home town], they were building a brand new high school. I wanted to be the first class in the new high school. I told my parents, I want to leave [my current school], go to a public high school in [my home town] and be part of the first class to enter the high school. So, my parents and I fought for it because we have another deaf person in the town. And the town cannot split us up for the expense. Because the other boy's mother wanted to keep him in [the current school not in my home town]. And my parents wanted to put me in [the school in my home town]. They have to pay for transportation, so they want one cost for both of us. We compromised that we would get a teacher for the deaf. I didn't even want one. I don't want no part of deaf teacher because I don't want them thinking that I'm dumb. I can do it. But this boy needed more help. (pause) I don't want to push him down, but I noticed this. So, I said "o.k., let's have the teacher for the deaf to help him and me too." And I have a note taker too. And that helped a lot. I appreciated the note taker. The teacher for the deaf, I don't know. She tried to push me down a little bit. I (She shakes her head "no."). I don't care for it. I went through normal high school classes with all the hearing people for all four years.

By reluctantly agreeing to the teacher of the deaf so that the other deaf student in her community could have that as part of his educational experiences, she was able to attend the public high school in her home town with hearing kids from her own neighborhood. Although she did not want her peers to think of her as "dumb," she agreed to this service so that she could be integrated into her home town's public school. This negotiating skill of knowing the politics of one's own education and when to push for one's rights occurs in many of these women's educational stories. Knowing when to push and when to hold back is a critical learned self-advocacy skill of these deaf women.

Wanting to be in the Deaf world

As I described in the section on parents' decisions about education, Stephanie's parents, in part because of seeing her older deaf sister struggle in the public school, allowed her to attend a manual state residential school for the deaf. Stephanie fought for herself to attend this school after she went on a field trip to see the public junior high. After this trip, she describes how she communicated and advocated for herself to her mother:

S: My mother asked me "how was your day?" "I don't like it." Mother said, "you don't like it, why?" I said, "now I understand what my sister is talking about, struggle." I was in junior high school, she was in high school. More scary to go to high school. She can't follow along. Remember that was back then in the 1950s, no interpreters, no support services. I asked her, "I don't want to go to that school." My mother said "o.k., do you have an idea where you want to go?" I said, "I want deaf institution." My mother asked me "how do you know about the deaf institution?" "Oh, you remember those people" (She puts her hands up and makes the "quotes" sign when she says "those people."). My friend told me, who used to come over my house and we play with each other. Sometimes, I would go over her house and sleep over. I remember you would not see them much. You know where they go? Deaf institution. Some of them want to go to college. Some of them play; me, nothing. Public school, people have no patience. Mother said, "so, you want to continue after you graduate?" I said "yes." But, later on my mother got the word that I could apply, go to the deaf institution. That's how, my mother do it for me.

Stephanie's experience is another example of the resistance work involved in self-advocacy. Instead of advocating to be with hearing students, Stephanie wanted to attend the manual state residential school for the deaf and resisted the "traditional" oral path for deaf women. Although she did not yet consider herself like "those people" or a member of the Deaf community, she also did not feel part of the hearing world. Her experiences with oralism and having an older deaf sister influenced her decision. The consequences of her act of resistance were that Stephanie was exposed to the Deaf community, learned ASL, and accepted herself as a deaf woman earlier than most of these women. It also influenced her decision to attend Gallaudet where there is a strong Deaf community.

Not NTID

Three of the five women who attended RIT had stories of how they wanted to attend RIT instead of NTID for a variety of reasons. The most common reasons were that they wanted the benefit of sign language interpreters, note takers, and a social connection to the Deaf community, but they also wanted a Bachelor's degree from a hearing college and not an Associate's degree, which is the highest degree granted by NTID. These factors suggest how the structure of higher education institutions played a role not only in their decision making about colleges, but how it also played a role in how they developed identities as deaf women. With few deaf colleges to choose from and many of the women not having attended a deaf school before, two women first chose to attend hearing colleges and then later transferred to RIT where they could have a Deaf community within a larger hearing college. Their stories illustrate another finding of this study which is that as the women struggled for their own individuality, they also sought educations which would provide them with greater access to job opportunities in a larger hearing society. The colleges became a site where they fought for access to these possibilities.

Heather, who spoke to school administrators when transferring from her hearing college to attend RIT, not NTID, wanted to ensure that she was admitted to RIT's Biology department before she entered the college:

> H: I want to get in first. I don't want to waste my time. It was a struggle at first. My mother helped me with the phone calls, but the chairperson of the Biology department had a conflict with what I want. Then, one of my friends that I met over the summer helped me to meet with the chairperson of the Biology department. And it works out. I get in. I took hearing class. A few deaf in Biology, signed class. But, note takers were really good because they got paid and there was training. They all should write as much information as possible. I needed that. I didn't want to go to NTID because it's very slow. It's AAS degree program. If I go there and take classes, I have to go to NTID first and I didn't want that. I wanted RIT. That's my goal.

Heather explains how getting her BA in Biology from RIT was her "goal" and how she, with the help of her friend and mother, was able to gain access to this goal. Heather, whose parents both went to college, also had the benefit of seeing older deaf peers attend NTID and then struggle to find jobs with an AAS degree or end up transferring to RIT to get their BA. Thus, in some ways, because of her place in history, Heather was able to see how, as a deaf woman, a degree from RIT would expand her opportunities. Later, she would get her MA in Statistics from RIT and work in the hearing world.

Marie, like Heather, wanted to attend RIT and not NTID so that she could get her BS in computer science and eventually work in that field. Unlike Heather, Marie only applied to NTID and then advocated for herself to get her degree from RIT:

> M: I picked NTID when I was a freshman in high school. The teacher for the deaf told my parents about it. My father decided to take me right away to look it over. I fell in love and I liked it. That's why I go. Right from the start. I didn't bother applying to any other colleges. My parents never went to college. My brothers and sisters all went through

college. So, I went in and I LOVED it. I would be able to communicate with a lot of deaf people. I was so much happier. BUT, when I go, I want to be in the hearing classroom. I wanted to go to RIT. I think that I always felt that deaf classes were always too easy, too simple. And I want a difficult. Challenge. I always thought hearing classroom was very challenging. And I went through NTID, it was easy, without even studying anything. My father said "why don't you go to NTID? Get your degree without any trouble. Maybe take one or two courses at RIT while you're at NTID." And I did. It helped me prepare for RIT full-time. I was planning on engineering or computer science. And my older brother recommended me to take computer science. He could see in the future that engineering needs to have computer skills. So, I start in computer skills and build my way if I want to include engineering.

Marie describes how she took her father's advice and then modified it by transferring to RIT. Her brother, who unlike her father, went to college, was able to give her additional advice about how she could market her degree. Getting her BS along with her desire to integrate herself with hearing people would eventually allow Marie opportunities to work in the hearing world, which she may not have had without these experiences.

Debbie decided to attend a hearing college due to the advice she got from an NTID admissions counselor who told her that she would do better at a hearing college:

D: I visited there and I met with the admissions counselor. He said, "there's only one other person who did better than you did." If he didn't tell me, I would have wasted my time there. I would have gone to NTID. Then, I would have moved to RIT. Some of my friends did that. They were socialized NTID and take classes at RIT. That would have been good for me, but the option was not explained clearly to me. And my friends were looking at colleges during that time. Because of a rubella epidemic, we were the same age. And they said "NTID, no." I went to Gallaudet, same thing. I dropped the whole thing and I applied to hearing colleges. And I got into all of them. [The hearing college I attended] was small. I decided that I want the community because I thought, I need the community to help me. I don't want to be a number. I said, "I've learned my lesson." I was at a small school, then I moved up to a bigger high school. I was fine because I've learned how to handle that.

Like Heather, Debbie shows us how her place in history, in some ways, allowed her to see how other deaf women fared at NTID. As she says, unlike Heather and Marie, her option to take classes at RIT as an NTID student was not explained clearly to her when she applied. This, along with the advice of the admissions counselor, influenced Debbie to advocate for herself to attend a small, private, religious, hearing college. Of all the women in this study, Debbie is the only woman to marry a hearing man. She is also one of only two women who works in the hearing world. In some ways, then, by attending the hearing college and not NTID, Debbie has become more integrated with the hearing world. All of the four women who attended hearing colleges for part of their undergraduate degrees, attended small, private institutions. Two of these institutions were all women and three of them were religiously affiliated. This along with Debbie's comments about attending a "small" school, shows that even those women who went to hearing colleges had to be strategic about which kinds of schools they attended. Thus, the educational opportunity for deaf women to successfully attend hearing colleges is more limited than the choices for hearing women.

"Lifetime Educators" in all Hearing Schools

All of the women in this study spoke of being "lifetime educators," which they saw as linked to their role as self-advocates. This occurred in a variety of settings in their educational careers. Being a lifetime educator often involved the work of negotiating with teachers, school administrators, and offices of support services to ensure their equal access to hearing classrooms. This learned skill often involved educating hearing people about what it was like to be deaf in a hearing classroom. As the women did this, they often developed a stronger sense of their deaf identities. Another major finding, then, of this study is that through the women's stories we can see how the work of gaining equal access to educational opportunities was often left up to the women. Without larger structural supports in place, such as interpreters, and a knowledge of deafness on behalf of the school personnel, the women had to develop strategies to fight for their rights. The following sections highlight some of the major strategies that the women used in these efforts.

The Overlap of being Self-Advocates and Lifetime Educators

Janice talked about her position of a lifetime educator and how it overlaps with being a self-advocate. She said, "I realize that I will always be a self advocate. That's a lifetime thing. That's not just for myself. When I advocate, I feel I'm educating others. I help ignorant people understand better." Janice's definition of the roles of a self-advocate and lifetime educator and how they overlap are critical in understanding the lives of these deaf women because the women use these skills in both their paid and unpaid work lives. As the women negotiated places for themselves, they moved back and forth from being in the deaf world, the hearing world, and places in between. One way of seeing how these roles develop is to look at the work that they do, such as negotiating with teachers in their hearing classrooms, to ensure their equal educational opportunities.

Negotiating with Teachers

Negotiating with teachers both in and outside of the classroom was something that all of these women experienced in their lives. At first glance, the role of a "lifetime educator" might appear to be a seemingly "natural" trait; however, once we uncover the work involved in this role, it becomes easier to see how most of these deaf women learn this skill at a very young age. Eight women also spoke of how their mothers also played a part in how they negotiated with their teachers, which suggests the often gendered nature of this work within family groups.

Kristen's story is an example of how one mother laid the groundwork for her daughter to develop the skills necessary of becoming a "lifetime educator." Kristen attended a hearing elementary school for one year which used "total communication" methods such as talking, signing, and written English so that she could make the transition to a private, religious hearing school that she attended from third until seventh grade. She tells a story of when she had to educate her teacher about her deafness:

> K: It took a toll, every day in school. My eyes would hurt from lip reading. Sometimes I would feel frustrated especially with oral quiz. "Did you say 'which' or 'what' or did you say?"(She pretends she's asking a teacher.) Particular word would look the same. I would put down as a guess. But, I did know the information. I would get it wrong. Then, I would get upset. I would talk to the teacher, the nun. She's sweet, so young. She said "no, you have to learn to watch me." But, she had no clue about my deafness. I'd say, "my homework, my studies, I work hard." When she would talk, she would look down and talk, her voice so soft. It's so difficult. At that point, I got so frustrated. I said, "may I be excused?" and I left and I went to the principal and I said, "please call my mother, I've had it." I said "Mom, I want to go home." When the teacher showed up, she saw my mother. She was like "what's going on?" My mother was excellent. She said "look, you two need to work it out. You know about her deafness, you have to trust her." [The teacher] looked at me, talking, fine. "What do you need?" I said, "write down the question on paper, on the board, whatever. Give me a

chance." She said, "o.k." She said "if you don't do well, then I know I was right." Well, it turned out she was wrong. I got most of the answers right. That was the first time, I realized, I knew stuff well. That was a turning point. I need to advocate myself (She signs something like "that was it."). And that was in fifth grade.

Kristen's story shows that the roles of a self-advocate and lifetime educator overlap. These are both learned skills, which develop over time in these deaf women's lives not only in their schools, but also within their families. Her story also illustrates how she not only had to advocate for her own education, but also for her own identity as a young deaf woman.

Debbie's story of educating the administrators and professors when she went to college after obtaining her Bachelor's degree is similar to Kristen's story in that it involves her being a lifetime educator. Debbie got her BSBA (Business Administration degree in Management Information Systems) at a large hearing university, which has a program for the deaf. She was the second deaf student to attend this university. Later, after working for some time, she got her MBA at a private, business, hearing college where she was the first deaf student to attend this college. She compares these two college experiences in the following story:

> D: At [the hearing university where I got my BSBA], it's a very good program. They set up everything for you. I just sign a piece of paper and the interpreter shows up. I do nothing. [The MBA] was an intensive program. I had to make sure that I get the interpreter and the support that I needed because [the hearing college where I got my MBA] never had a deaf student so I had to educate them what I need. But at [the hearing college], I did some work to make sure that I get an interpreter for all my classes, note taking services. There was a lot of collaboration with [the hearing college]. It was a financial risk for me to go there because I had to pay and [the hearing college] had to pay for the interpreter. We worked together to make this work. At [the hearing college], I had ninety-nine percent of my classes interpreted. Study groups interpreted. Sometimes not. Depending on what I needed.

Debbie, by highlighting the subtle yet important differences between her two educational experiences, shows that by being the first deaf student to attend the college, she not only had to "educate" the school about what she needed for support, but she also had to know when to prioritize her needs.

Similar to Marie's act of resistance in high school when she accepted the support service of having a teacher of the deaf so that she could attend the hearing school in her home town, Debbie was also aware of the politics of her education and knew when and when not to push for services. Debbie's story also shows how self-advocacy and being a lifetime educator overlap. By knowing when to push for services and when to hold back, Debbie was able to negotiate for services at this college as well as educate them about her needs as a deaf student.

Janice, who is currently working on her certificate in Education Administration, is for the first time in her educational career, at a hearing institution. She is the only deaf student at the college and has interpreters; however, she communicated to me that there are some nights that she will "go home and cry" because her eyes are so tired from watching her interpreter and lip reading her peers:

> J: In this one class with this teacher, I realize I had to educate my professor about me. I have to tell him what I need in the role with the interpreter. I wrote him a long letter. I showed the professor. He was like (She gives a look of shock.). He wanted me to share the letter with everyone in the class. It was good. That really helped me understand what it was like for deaf students who were mainstreamed. It's still hard. There's only one interpreter and there is lag time. Back and forth, back and forth.
>
> C: But, I think it's good for the class.
>
> J: Yes, many of them will become administrators, so they need to know.

Janice's story of educating not only her professor, but also the class, suggests that being a lifetime educator is a skill that Janice has learned over the years by doing work such as negotiating with her teachers. As with many of the women, her position of a lifetime educator also overlaps with her being a self-advocate because her work has become a type of activism. Her example illustrates this because she is, as part of this class experience, able to educate people who will later hold positions where they might have an influence on deaf students.

Janice, without my asking, gave me a copy of the letter. As someone who relies heavily on communication and visual media, Janice gave me this piece of "data" which articulates her experiences in ways which our interview, due to our language miscommunications, might not reveal. It suggests that she might see our interview as an opportunity to further educate me as well as other audiences about the Deaf community. An excerpt of the letter is as follows:

February 11, 2002

Dear Professor,

I want to let you know how much I enjoy your class and to share a little bit about myself. I believe I am the first Deaf student you have had in your classroom. I was born into a Deaf family, and English is my second language. To this day, my only exposure to it comes in the form of the printed word, or English text.

I do want to take this opportunity to explain my experience as the only Deaf person in class as well as one who uses interpreters. I have been assigned two of the best interpreters in the Rochester area and I trust I am being given an accurate interpretation of class lecture and discussion. However, there are many factors involved that I feel the need to share. The process of interpreting requires a lag time because interpreters are going from one language to another. Interpreters listen to the English, process it in their minds and then produce it manually in American Sign Language (ASL). Because there isn't always an equivalent meaning in ASL, some things end up filtered by the interpreter's choices.

Because ASL is a visual language, I must keep my eyes on the interpreter at all times. The class size is larger than ideal, so following so much continual conversation doesn't allow for a distinction between voices. This is certainly not a complaint. This is simply the process of interpretation. However, I have a suggestion that may be helpful for all the students in the class. If turn taking was done by raising one's hand, it would allow me to quickly see for myself who is speaking and give me a more personal, one on one experience. The interpreter can then have a chance to include pauses between speakers. It also allows my eyes to "breathe." I understand that the dynamics of this course involves banter and heavy discussion. I am not trying to squelch that. I certainly don't want you to change your style. My goal here is twofold–1) for me to get more equal access in the classroom and 2) for you to have a more clear understanding of the process.

With the above mentioned constraints, it becomes difficult to internalize ALL the information I am trying to process in the classroom. I write this not to use Deafness as an excuse but to clarify the additional weight I am faced with. My progress may not be as great as I would like. I am accustomed to a visually oriented, direct educational environment. I know it is my responsibility to work within the boundaries I am faced with and to do whatever it takes to achieve success in the class. That is my role. It is my hope, however, that you as the Professor as well as the other students can see this as an opportunity to "ennoble" the class experience. How fitting that we can hopefully take this opportunity as one of many potential ways to build a foundation to educational leadership.

Janice sees her involvement in the class as a way to build "educational leadership," which shows that she, by advocating for herself, is educating not only her professor and peers, but also future generations of administrators. Janice's experiences seem linked to her current work as a Director at a manual state residential school for the deaf where she works on mentoring and training teachers of the deaf. In this position, she is able to work in the Deaf community as well as continue her role of a lifetime educator and activist by preparing both deaf and hearing teachers of the deaf.

"Coping" as a Strategy of Integration

All of these women talked about ways in which they tried to integrate themselves socially into their educational environments. This was particularly true for each of them when they attended hearing schools or were mainstreamed. Many did this by developing strategies such as being outgoing, observing other children, and by participating in sports and extra curricular activities.

Being Outgoing as a Strategy

Debbie, when reflecting on her family while growing up, discussed how she was more outgoing than her brother and sister as a way of "coping" with her deafness:

> D: A lot of people say that I'm the most outgoing of the three of us. I would just meet people. I had to learn to do it. It's a way of coping my deafness, meeting people. If it was the other way around, if they were doing things for me, it'd be (She signs "different.").

Debbie's sentiments illustrate how coping with her deafness by being outgoing was a skill which she learned while growing up in her all hearing family and while attending hearing schools. Her strategy of being outgoing as a way of coping with her "disability" also became a way in which she advocated for herself as well as helped her siblings and became a role model for them. Debbie's work experiences, primarily in the hearing world and with a Deaf activist group, seem connected to her early experiences of learning to be more outgoing in various sectors of her life.

Observing as a Strategy

Another strategy that six of these deaf women used was to learn to observe others in their educational surroundings both in and outside of the classroom. Instead of being outgoing in her educational and home settings like Debbie, Heather described how she used the strategy of observing as a way of dealing with her "disability" not only with her peers, but also in her mainstreamed classroom:

> H: I was shy growing up. I'm different now. I was observing other kids, other people. I was best with one on one or two people. Not a group. In school, I would just sit there, look at the teacher. Pttt (She makes a motion with her hand over her head like information is going past her.). Just look around. I got no information. I'm not a good lip reader. My favorite class was math because he would write on the board. And I spent a lot of time looking at the numbers figuring it out. The teacher explained, but (She makes a sign by waving her hand and shaking her head "no," which looks like she didn't listen.) I figured it out myself. And I would come up with the right answer that was on the board. That was exciting. So, math was my favorite subject. In the textbook most of the answers were in the textbook or I would read the book in English.

Heather describes how in social settings at school, she would observe the other kids to try to follow the conversation. She mentioned that she did have hearing friends, but did better in one on one settings rather than in a group of hearing people where she was not able to follow along. Like three of the other women, Heather spoke of how she excelled in math rather than English because she could visually see the numbers on the board as well as teach herself from the textbook rather than rely as much on lip reading her teacher. These experiences would later influence Heather's educational opportunities where got her MA in Statistics. Lastly, she mentions how she is "different" now implying that she is more outgoing. Her involvement and exposure to the Deaf community and ASL later in life, then, also affected her communication style and sense of herself as a deaf woman.

Participating in Sports Activities

Another strategy in which four of these women tried to become socially integrated in their educational settings was to participate in sports activities. Again, this became more critical for those that were mainstreamed into mostly hearing schools or attended hearing colleges. Kristen describes how, much like Debbie, by being outgoing was involved in various sports in high school to keep herself "in the group." She said, "I was involved in sports. Tennis. Volleyball. Kickball. I was involved with so many. It was the only way I could get myself involved. Know what's going on. I kept myself in the group. Because you know with my deafness I could miss so much." Kristen understood just how critical it was for her to feel socially connected to her peers at her all hearing high school. One of the consequences of this was that Kristen chose a hearing college where she also played tennis; however, after struggling without interpreters or note takers, she ended up transferring to RIT where she could be more socially integrated with the Deaf community as well as where she could also thrive academically.

Debbie discussed how she was able to "fit in" at her hearing college because of her involvement with the swim team:

> D: I was able to fit in because I was involved in the swimming team all four years. In high school, I was doing three sports a year, so I was able to socialize with people that way. I continued that in college. The swimming season was from August until the end of March. I had my college experience through swimming. It was fun. I was part of the team. That was good.

Debbie's story, much like Kristen and many of the other mothers, shows how her strategy of playing sports helped her to socially integrate better with her hearing peers. These two examples of tennis and swimming also suggest that while being part of a sports team was an important factor, examples of women on teams at their hearing schools where lots of verbal communication were required were less common. This can be seen in Marie's example of her extra curricular involvement in her hearing high school.

Extra Curricular Activities and Integration

As with being part of a sports team, taking part in extra curricular activities for any student is a way to integrate oneself socially into an educational environment. For these deaf women, it became a critical piece in understanding not only their educational histories, but also in understanding how they saw themselves as deaf women. Marie, similar to Debbie, "tried to fit into the group" by becoming a rifle twirler:

> M: I tried to get involved in after school activities. Hopefully, that will increase my involvement with the hearing kids. I was a rifle twirler. I wanted to be a majorette twirler. But the woman that was in charge of the band recommended me to do the rifle. I said, "no. I want to be a bigger part of the girls." But the rifle was maybe only four or five girls.

I said, "o.k., so I'll go for it." So, I went for it and I did it for three years. I LOVED it. So, I didn't do the majorette twirling.

This story of Marie joining the rifle team shows the complexity of her experience in high school of trying to socially integrate with hearing kids. The band leader dissuades her from being a majorette twirler because the group was too large and communication might be more difficult; however, she was able to be a rifle twirler where there were only four or five girls on the squad and she enjoyed this experience as well as got to know members of her class. Like most of these women, her way of coping with the stigma of her "disability" in an all hearing school was to socially integrate herself as much as possible by resisting various barriers. By learning this skill of "coping" early on she was negotiating her place as a deaf woman in the deaf and hearing worlds.

COMMUNICATION IN PERSONAL RELATIONSHIPS AND CURRENT FAMILIES

Between Worlds and Communication and Personal Relationships

Another aspect of these women's lives was how they developed both romantic relationships and friendships while negotiating being in between worlds along with their identities as deaf women. Debbie is the only one in this study who is married to a hearing man to whom she taught sign language so that they might communicate more easily. Debbie's relationship with her hearing husband was unlike the experiences of the other nine women of this study who are all currently married or were at one time to deaf men. Four women had stories about how they ended relationships with hearing men or men who identified differently than they with the Deaf community. The partner choices of these women, which involved issues of communication and cultural identities, were another place where these women negotiated their deaf identities and places for themselves. These relationships then later influenced whether the women worked in the hearing or deaf world.

Romantic Relationships with Hearing Men

Carol, who made such a decision, describes when she decided to end a relationship with her hearing boyfriend:

Carol: I had a hearing boyfriend in tenth through twelfth grade. So, I'm always with him. Comfortable with him. He (pause) well, I don't really sign much [back then].

C: What was it like talking to him? Was it just oral?

Carol: Yeah, oral. He's easy to lip read. The more I know him, I'm used to his mouth movements. But, the hardest part was that I have some deaf friends. He doesn't know what's going on. When I'm with him with his friends, I'm lost. So, I went to college. When I went to college, we broke up. But, we kept in touch. He wanted to hold on to me. And I said, "let's see how it goes." So, when I went to college, I was "oh, cool." Same communication, comfortable signing. And I, of course, met men there. Same. I feel more comfortable. But, the deafness didn't bother him. He "Oh, it's fine." But, I know we have a problem later on. Suppose we have his friends (She makes a motion like "get together, but have trouble understanding one another."). I'll be left out and he'll be left out with my friends signing. He can get along with friends who talk like me, but I have some friends who can't speak well.

C: They're more ASL.

Carol: Yeah. So, I don't want to be in conflict. But, suppose we have children and they're all hearing. I'd be left out. The more I dated deaf men, I feel more comfortable. I have a better relationship with them. If he knows sign, maybe things would be different. I don't know.

Since an ideology of American culture is to have a partnership with open communication, Carol struggled with the relationship she had with her hearing boyfriend and the potential challenges they might have if they had a family together. After attending NTID, learning ASL, and being exposed to men in the Deaf community, Carol made the personal and also political decision to end the relationship. Her cultural shift in her identity as Deaf, when she attended NTID, influenced how she thought of her future family and her position in this family as a deaf woman. Her experiences of growing up oral in an all hearing family and sometimes feeling left out even today also seemingly affected her desire to be included in her own future family group. Both Carol and her husband work at an oral state residential school for the deaf where they have been able to develop personal and professional relationships, mostly with members of the Deaf community.

Romantic Relationships with Deaf Men

The women also spoke of relationships that they had with deaf men and how there were differences *among* these experiences. Teresa, although she now considers herself Deaf, grew up in a strong oral environment. She explains why she ended her relationship with her Deaf manualist boyfriend when she worked at an oral state residential school for the deaf where she could not use sign:

T: I was becoming active with [members of the Deaf community]. Sign, talk, sign talk. Two different worlds going back and forth. There was a man in the group, so we started dating then. Learning sign. Going to work was going to a different world. (laughs). I worked with teenage girls. They asked me all kinds of questions about my dating life. One time they saw one of the boys I was dating. "Oh!" (She pretends the girls are looking at him.). "He can't talk?" "No. He can sign." "Tell me some signs." "I can't." (Teresa pretends she is having a conversation with the girls. She gives me a look of frustration, but is also smiling.). So, I dated for a while and that summer I broke up with the guy because I was concerned about our communication. He was a deaf manual guy. He couldn't speak. And he didn't go to college. And he was a lot of fun to be with, but I had to think of other things. So, after two years we broke up.

Despite learning some signs, Teresa was not allowed to use sign language in her paid work environment, which affected how she thought of herself as deaf as well as how she negotiated her personal relationships. Unlike the other women in this study, she did not have large exposure to the Deaf community or learn ASL until she later married, had her three children, and moved to Rochester. Since her cultural shift and perception of her identity as a deaf woman came later than the other women in this study, this influenced her decision to date other deaf men and eventually marry a deaf man, who like her, was raised in an oral environment and was also college educated. Her story also points to how her work environment influenced how she thought of herself as deaf, which prompted her to pursue relationships with men of a similar world or experience.

Friendships with Hearing Mothers

Another area where the women discussed the importance of going back and forth between two worlds was in their friendships. Although not against having hearing friends, all of the women in this study mentioned that their close friends were deaf. One exception to this was Janice who described a story of how her friendship developed with a hearing woman whom she met in her graduate program at Gallaudet:

J: In my Master's program, looking, some hearing students. At that time, it was like "hey, what are they doing here?" Gallaudet, deaf. Hearing? I guess I was going through, anxious, "oh, hearing, why are they here?" I became friends with one hearing woman. It changed my whole life. I guess she helped me to understand. I feel that way because of my experience growing up. Voice, voice, voice. At Gallaudet, it was like (She makes an expression that looks like "relief."). Then, Master's, "hearing?" (She gives a look of shock.). Not all hearing people are like that. She and I became close friends. She made me accept hearing people. She's an interpreter and was an interpreter for our wedding.

After growing up in an all deaf family where she was raised orally and then later at Gallaudet identifying with the Deaf community, Janice had developed certain perceptions and stereotypes of hearing people as well as a strong Deaf identity. This hearing woman, who was being trained as an interpreter and knew ASL, could more easily communicate with Janice. As Janice negotiated what it meant to be a deaf woman, in some ways, so too was this hearing woman negotiating what it meant to be in between worlds. Language, then, plays a major role in how these deaf women made political decisions about their friendships, which influenced them in their family groups and how they saw themselves as deaf women. Although she did have this one bilingual hearing friend and was educated orally, Janice, who grew up in an all deaf family and whose husband and children are all deaf, made the decision to work in the deaf world where she might more easily communicate with her colleagues.

Between Worlds and Communication in Current Families

The following examples point to the places where these women explicitly discussed being "between worlds" in their positions as wives and mothers as well as how they interacted with other mothers in their communities. As Carol's story at the beginning of this chapter suggests, their personal relationships and mothering experiences are interrelated. Carol mentioned that she sought a partner who was deaf so that she would not feel isolated in her future family. For the deaf women of this study, it became critical to have personal connections at home to help fight the isolation they might feel as part of a larger hearing society.

Communication with Deaf Husbands

As mentioned earlier, all of the women in this study were married to deaf men, except for Debbie who taught her hearing husband sign language. Although four women spoke of relationships with deaf men as often easier than relationships with hearing men, there were also important differences *within* these experiences and how they related to their experiences as wives. The differences within the Deaf community influenced how Beth saw herself as a wife and mother to their two hearing children:

B: My husband and I, we just recently separated. He's hard of hearing
and I'm really profoundly deaf and he speaks really well. So he could
speak with the kids and he would rarely sign with them. And me, I
needed him to sign all the time. Their father and I don't see a lot of
other people everyday. We don't go to the Deaf club. We don't really
hang out at different Deaf organizations. When I sign sometimes, [my
daughter] doesn't understand me. So, I'll speak one or two words and
then she'll understand what I mean. So, we use the combination of
speech, signs and finger spelling, to make sure they understand what
I'm saying. That's how we communicate in this house.

Beth, as a profoundly Deaf woman, and perhaps since she does not see
many people in her work setting or participate much in social events with
the Deaf community, especially desires to have a family that can easily communicate and that uses sign language. Also, Beth, who works as an Assistant Professor at NTID, has a strong Deaf identity as her paid work reflects
how she sees being a deaf woman. Beth's idea of herself as a deaf woman
influences her mothering experiences. Since her hard of hearing husband
was using spoken English with their hearing daughter, Beth shows how this
led to a struggle in communication with her daughter. This became a dis-
agreement between Beth and her husband and was a seemingly contribut-
ing factor in their recent separation. Beth's example shows how the
"success" of her family group became disrupted when her family was
unable to go back and forth between these two worlds. Having a partnership where both people have similar political views of what it means to be
deaf and experiences of deafness relates to how the women communicate
and define themselves within their families.
    When asked if her husband is hard of hearing or deaf, Carol
described how she and her deaf husband work together as a team to raise
their hearing daughter by stating, "He hears more than me. Um (laughs)
. . . I don't know, we're very much similar. I know he's deaf. He doesn't
hear high frequency. I don't hear low frequency. It's like team." Carol,
while hesitating to categorize her husband as hearing or deaf, instead discusses his sensory ability as one might discuss a personality trait to illustrate how they work together in their positions as husband and wife and as
a team. For Carol, part of the invisible work of having a successful partnership with her husband involved working as a team to effectively communicate in a larger hearing society. Carol resisted putting her husband and
herself in a category of either deaf or hearing. Instead, by describing their
"disabilities" as working together as part of a team, she shows how being
deaf is an asset to their relationship as a couple. By both working as a team

and thinking of their deafness as an ability became strategies for these deaf women as they worked, as Carol's story shows, to resist definitions of themselves as "disabled."

Other Friendships with Hearing Mothers

While none of the five Rochester women described current friendships with hearing mothers, three of the Boston women did discuss some of the challenges they found when trying to connect with their deaf women friends who were also mothers and lived far away. These three women in the Boston group also spoke of feeling somewhat isolated from the Deaf community and shared some of the challenges and successes of making friends with hearing mothers in their communities. Since Boston is a place where the Deaf community is more spread out than in a place like Rochester, location or community has an influence on the daily mothering experiences of these deaf women and the ways in which they negotiate their identities as being in between worlds in their paid work experiences.

Carol describes when her hearing daughter wanted to go to an all hearing Halloween party:

> Carol: Before I had my daughter, I was more involved [with the Deaf community]. I had friends. When my daughter was born, I'm more half, half. Because what happens is she wants to go to her friend's school. It was a Halloween party. I said "fine." And there's another party at the [oral state residential school for the deaf where I work]. I usually take her there because she's younger. I said, "do you want to go?" She said, "no." Her friends over there. So, I take her there. I want her to have a good childhood growing up with her parents. But, sometimes it's nice. I have a [hearing] friend who has the same age child, so we go and they keep us company. There's one. When she was younger, she had a play date. My husband stayed and tried to communicate with her friend's mom. It's hard. It depends. This one woman, I like her a lot, but the other it was like (She makes a sign like "it was hard to negotiate.").

Carol has had some feelings of isolation from the Deaf community after the birth of her hearing daughter. As part of her work of mothering, she goes back and forth between the worlds of the deaf and hearing to ensure that her hearing daughter is part of both of these worlds. This seemingly invisible work influenced how Carol negotiated her own identity as a deaf mother. Also, since the first Halloween party she mentioned was where she worked in the deaf world, this affected how she had to reconcile her identity as a Deaf woman in her position as a mother and as a worker. By choosing to send her daughter to the hearing Halloween party, she was making a decision that her family's community was not restricted to members of the Deaf community.

Despite being her daughter's Girl Scout Troop leader and working with hearing mothers, Marie, also a Boston mother, shared some similar feelings of isolation:

> M: Sometimes right now my relationship with hearing people around here (She points outside her house.) is not the same. I kind of miss the deaf environment. Communicate with [deaf] friends. But they live so far. It's difficult for me to stay around because of the kids. The kids like to be with their friends. I want them to have that opportunity. So, I kind of hold back with that part, but I knew that I would catch up to it in the next phase in my life.

While part of the work of mothering is being able to connect socially with other mothers in one's community, the experiences of these deaf women illustrate how this may become a challenge for some of the deaf women who lived in all hearing communities. Also, both Carol's and Marie's examples illustrate another strategy of these women, which was how they worked to integrate their hearing children into the hearing world.

CONCLUSION

For the deaf women in this study, discovering or acknowledging deafness, their parents' decisions about their educations, and their own decisions about education had a profound affect not only on their educational experiences, but also on how they thought of themselves as deaf women. Although the experiences of growing up oral, manual, or a combination of both differed in some ways for these women, each struggled to communicate in a larger hearing society while developing and maintaining their identities as deaf women. This chapter has also shown the places where these women and their parents resisted the various obstacles and stigmas they encountered in their educational experiences.

One major finding of this chapter is that as the women made decisions about their educations, they were struggling also for a sense of place. This description of going back and forth between worlds or cultures echoes literature written by women of color who describe their experiences as a kind of "'world'-travelling" and border crossing (Ahmed, 2000; Anzaldua, 1990; Lugones, 1990). As members of a linguistic minority, then, these deaf women struggled to both learn and then use their native language, ASL, in both their school and family settings while finding a sense of place for themselves. The schools and colleges they attended became key sites for where they fought for their rights as part of the Deaf community and in their positions as a cultural, ethnic, and linguistic minorities. Another finding was that, as the women struggled for their own individuality, they sought educations, as most do, that might provide them with access to job opportunities in a larger hearing society. Despite this, they were often tracked into working in the deaf world.

A third major finding was that in order to gain access to these opportunities in their educational experiences, the women developed three major strategies to integrate themselves into both hearing and deaf educational settings. These strategies included being self-advocates, lifetime educators, and, as one woman described, learning to "cope" with their deafness in an effort to become part of a larger social group. The work of gaining this access, however, was mostly left up to the individual women. Without things in place such as interpreters, note takers, or knowledge about the Deaf community, the women had to know when to hold back and when to advocate for themselves. In this way, the decisions that they made regarding their educations can be viewed as political as they were also making political decisions about their own cultural identities as Deaf women. If they advocated to attend a school for the deaf that encouraged manualism, they were seen as part of the larger Deaf community; however, if they attended all hearing schools, they were often seen as outsiders in the larger hearing setting.

The ways in which the women did the work of resistance shaped their educational opportunities and family lives. How and when these women learned ASL and were exposed to members of the Deaf community also played a role in their educational opportunities. These findings suggest that, due to wanting to be socially integrated and succeed in school, many of these women navigate toward or are encouraged to get their educations in the deaf world. This resonates with DeVault (1999) who has argued that race or ethnicity, while perhaps not affecting career choice directly, plays a role in both choosing and being channeled into a particular profession. In a similar way, these bilingual deaf women, because of their perceived abilities, chose, but were also channeled into particular schools, which made their educational opportunities more limited than hearing women.

Growing up oral may seemingly privilege these deaf women as they are more able to negotiate their way in a larger hearing society; however, as I will later discuss, they are constantly doing the work of self-advocacy and educating hearing people about their deafness in their work settings. Educational institutions, the medical system, and the employment sector, then greatly affect and in some cases, limit the choices and opportunities of these deaf women's educational and work experiences. Although an education at a deaf university might also seemingly privilege these women to obtain jobs in the hearing world, because of their experiences of identifying with the Deaf community, they are drawn and sometimes even recruited by employers to the Deaf world where it is often easier to communicate and where they might feel more socially connected in their work settings.

Chapter Four will first uncover how these women continue to use some of the learned skills that they have developed as part of their educational experiences and how these women, particularly those with deaf children, teach these skills to their children so they might also learn to negotiate their own educations. The skills of self-advocacy and being a lifetime educator, then, relate to both their paid and unpaid work lives as well as their educational histories. As with their own experiences with ASL and members of the Deaf community, many of these women and their husbands also make important decisions about how they would educate and communicate with their children within their family groups in the context of a hearing world. These experiences also influenced how these women as well as their families see themselves.

Chapter Four
Motherwork, Deafness, and the Role of Activism in Families

This chapter investigates the mothering experiences of college educated deaf women in the context of a larger hearing society and connects these experiences to their current family lives. As suggested in chapter three, the educational experiences, early family life experiences, and personal relationships of these deaf women influenced their work as mothers. This chapter is organized into two sections which include children and communication and decisions about children's education. Each of these sections uncovers various kinds of visible and invisible work that these deaf women do as they continue negotiating their identities and places in the world. Their stories suggest that these experiences help shape how these women do the work of mothering and how they see themselves as deaf women. The findings of this chapter specifically point to how these women do the invisible work of integrating themselves into their extended families and communities, how they make political decisions about their choices of language as well as educating their children, how they work to "normalize" their experiences as deaf mothers, and how, through their activism, they recognize various obstacles in their lives and work to resist them.

This chapter then also highlights some of these challenges that the women face in making decisions about how to communicate with and educate their hearing or deaf children and in how they balance their roles as mothers with their activism. Although these obstacles do exist, these women work to resist these barriers by teaching their children and extended families about self-advocating and lifetime educating people about the deaf. These learned skills, as described in chapter three, also then become a part of the various strategies these women use in their work of mothering.

CHILDREN AND COMMUNICATION

Seven of the women in this study have hearing children, while Kristen, Janice, and Ellen have children who are all deaf. The work of mothering, as with all women, began at the time of pregnancy when these women visited doctors who assisted them with their deliveries. Husbands influenced the mothering as well, especially regarding discussions of whether parents wanted hearing or deaf children and in making decisions about how they would communicate not only in their own family groups, but also with members of their extended families. Making decisions about whether to use American Sign Language (ASL), Sign Exact English (SEE), oral methods, or a mixture of communication methods in their families was part of the invisible work that these college educated deaf women did in their work as mothers.

Self-Advocates and Lifetime Educators: Experiences with Doctors

One place where these college educated deaf women advocated for themselves and educated people about the Deaf community was in their interaction with members of the medical community. The process of negotiating care with their doctors while they were pregnant was of great importance to the women's experiences of motherhood. All of the women relied on lip reading to understand their doctors, which, in most cases, as they reported, worked well enough. There were other times, however, when these women had to advocate for themselves and educate members of the medical community about their deafness. One example is where Marie developed a strategy to dispel stigmas and stereotypes about what it means to be deaf. After hearing this woman's story, we have to wonder about some of the opportunities that were missed in the women's experiences with members of the medical community.

"I can think"

As a mother of four hearing children, Marie described a turning point in her life when she needed an interpreter in her doctor's office:

> M: If I go to the doctor's office, one on one I'm o.k. When it comes to a group, I need an interpreter. I needed an interpreter at that point because I needed an anesthesia doctor. That anesthesia doctor (She makes a sign that looks like "over my head" and shakes her head.). This doctor I don't understand at all. I have no clue. I asked my husband and he had a hard time understanding him too. So, they finally got an interpreter last minute. My regular doctor couldn't get over how the interpreter works. And he was shocked that I can say whatever I want through the interpreter. And after

M: that exposure he became very close with me. He'd talk about different things. He'd pull up his chair and sit and talk to me like a friend.

C: With the interpreter there or?

M: No, without the interpreter. I really think that he realized that I was able to do a lot of things. I was intelligent. I can think.

Marie was later able to understand her options about giving birth, which gave her a greater sense of control with that pregnancy as well as with the births of her other children. Having the interpreter present helped reduce some of the stereotypes that her regular doctor may have had about her abilities not only as a deaf woman, but also as a deaf mother. By insisting on gaining a full understanding, which also resulted in redefining her relationship with her doctor to include friendship, Marie was doing the invisible work of mothering, which included advocating for herself and educating her doctor about her deafness as well as about her needs as a mother. This work was incredibly important to both Marie and her children as it would have a later influence on her mothering experiences.

No Cochlear Implants

Doctors suggested to one of the three mothers in this study who has deaf children that she give her daughter a cochlear implant, which suggests that, according to the women, the doctors viewed deafness as unhealthy. Although Ellen and her husband consider their daughter Kate Deaf, since she was technically born hard of hearing, she would, according to the medical community, be a viable candidate for this surgery. Ellen remembers the experience as follows:

E: When Kate was born. Make me and my husband thrilled. Surprise. Happy. I feel good because it's easy to communicate, family. It's good. And the doctor offered for Kate a cochlear implant. I said no. Because the family is Deaf. We prefer that. But we will get her hearing aids. Because she's hard of hearing. Reads lips too. It improved her lip reading. When my mother and father visited the hospital and Kate was tested for hearing and we found out that she was deaf, my father upset. But now my mother and father look (She points to Kate who has just come over to her.) and like "wow. She's good, smart, manualist." But I can't sign well when I was a little girl. Big difference between us. Understand?

C: Yes, you were saying that when Kate was born, your father, your parents were upset.

E: My parents were not upset, they were just very surprised. "Wow. Deaf. Can't believe." Peter and I, that's my daughter. Make my father, "wow." (She points to Peter and seems to sign two people arguing. It looks like Peter and her father disagreed and may have fought over if Kate should get a cochlear implant.)

Ellen's story shows that by resisting a cochlear implant for her daughter, she was actively resisting the idea that deafness is a disability or something that needs to be fixed. Instead, she and Peter viewed Kate's deafness as an asset to their family so that they could communicate more easily in their native language of ASL. The decision to reject a cochlear implant for her daughter, as well as to incorporate some oral methods of communication, points to another example of a kind of invisible work of deaf mothering. This work influenced how these women continually negotiate their own deaf identities as well the identities of their children and families.

Wanting Deaf or Hearing Children

With the exception of Debbie, all of the women in this study were currently married or had been married to deaf men. Four of the women discussed if they wanted deaf or hearing children with their husbands prior to the birth of their children, while the six other mothers did not. Only Janice and Ellen expressed preferences for their children to be born deaf while no one said that they specifically wanted hearing children. Kristen, Janice, and Ellen, the three mothers who had all deaf children, expressed great pride in having deaf children. Six of the ten women also said that they did not have strong preferences for their children to be born hearing or deaf; however, they did want their children to be "healthy." This shows how these women thought of being born deaf as well as hearing as healthy.

"If I had blue eyes"

Janice's story of the birth of her deaf son sheds some light on the connections between wanting a deaf child who is also healthy:

J: When my son was born, I thought he was hearing. So, we were heart broken. Oh, my God, what do we do with a hearing child? (laughs) But, because we're deaf, it would be a good idea for him to go through evaluations. So, one evaluation said he's normal, another said no. It took seventeen evaluations before his hearing loss was official. I was born deaf. Our children helped us to understand how our husband became deaf. With my two children it was a progressive hearing loss. Their hearing loss is different from many deaf people. My husband didn't really understand how he became deaf. His parents told him he became deaf when he was four. Nerve deafness. But, that helped my husband to understand it was the same.

C: Now, why was it so important to have deaf children?

J: It's normal for parents to want to have children that are the same as them. If I had blue eyes, I would want my children to have the same. My parents are deaf. I have a wonderful relationship with them. I want that. It's important that they're healthy.

Janice, in explaining to me why she had a preference for having deaf children, shows that "deafness" is a physical attribute, such as blue eyes, rather, than a "disability." Coming from an all deaf family, she mentions how this "attribute" of being deaf would help her to develop a similar bond with her own children that she had with her deaf parents, seemingly because they would speak the same language. By learning how their children became deaf, Janice and her husband came to a greater understanding of her husband's deafness, which aided him in developing his own identity. By stating that it is "normal" for parents to want children who are like them, Janice also developed a strategy of "normalizing" her experience as a college educated deaf mother and resisted seeing herself and her family as different from hearing families.

Being Born "Healthy"

Another mother who wanted her daughter to be born healthy, but who did not express a strong preference for her child to be deaf or hearing, was Carol:

C: Did you and your husband prefer to have a deaf kid?

Carol: (She signs but does not say verbally "didn't matter.") We accept the way. If she's deaf, we know what to do because we were too. Hearing, we accept. We don't care as long as she's healthy. That's important. When she was born, we're happy to have her.

Unlike Janice, Carol's daughter was born hearing, however, she still considers her to be healthy. One can see that these women's ideas of a "healthy" child included not only deaf children, but also hearing children. This example illustrates how these women were continually defining what it meant to be deaf, hearing, or somewhere in between. It also shows how, as mothers, they negotiated their ideas about what it meant to be healthy, disabled, deaf, and hearing.

How will we communicate?

All of the women spoke of how they, along with their husbands, communicated with their deaf and hearing children. Seven of the women taught their children ASL while also using other methods of communication. The other three mothers, Teresa, Debbie, and Marie, primarily used their voices, some home signs, and relied on lip reading. How to communicate with one's child became a key part of the often invisible mothering work of these deaf women and these decisions influenced how they and their children thought of themselves as deaf, hearing, or somewhere in between. Three of the women said that they had dialogues with their husbands about making these decisions before the children were born. All of the women spoke of making decisions about communication as they raised their children and how they watched them "picking up" languages and going "back and forth" from their different languages.

Discussions Before the Children are Born

Stephanie's story of how she and her husband decided to sign to their three hearing children illustrates this work of a college educated deaf mother. Because of her experience in her family growing up where they primarily used oral methods, Stephanie had a particular view of how she wanted to communicate with her own children:

> S: From my experience with my family, I continued on with some, but not all. I want my children to be part of us. So, from day one, when each child was born, I started signing. Voice was mostly shut off. I never looked at my children whether they're hearing or deaf. I looked at who they are. That's Sara. That's Maureen. That's Robbie. I want to teach them [sign language], but [my husband] doesn't care. Doesn't matter to him. To me, it was important. So, o.k. "Hearing, deaf, how you feel?" (She pretends it is her and her husband talking.) We feel fine. "If it's hearing and speak how you feel?" He said, "Fine, but hope the children can sign." I said, "No problem, we can teach them."

By growing up with a mix of hearing and deaf family members and being deaf herself, Stephanie saw the importance of using not just home signs, but specifically teaching her children ASL. Experiences growing up influenced how each of these women made decisions about how to communicate with their children, especially for those seven women who taught their children ASL. In eight of the ten cases, the women spoke of initiating this conversation about how to communicate with their children with their husbands. This suggests that the work of making decisions about communication was also gendered and seen as part of the position of being a deaf mother.

Do What Comes "Natural"

Seven women did not discuss with their husbands how they would communicate with their children before they were born. Marie and her husband decided to do what came naturally:

> C: Did you and your husband talk at all before they were born about teaching them sign or did you not talk about that?
>
> M: (She shakes her head "no.") I knew it would come natural. Normal. I don't think about what we should do. We talk more about what school they should go. Public or private school. It's just a normal conversation.

Marie actively resists describing the decisions about communicating with her four hearing children as different or abnormal from the decisions of hearing mothers. Her use of the word "normal" points to how she and her husband also did not construct deafness as a "disability." Marie's view is an example of how these women negotiated their and their children's identities as deaf, hearing, or somewhere in between. It also suggests that this work is an ongoing process. Further, one can see from her story that she, as with many of these mothers, had developed a strategy to "normalize" her experiences and resist being seen as different in a larger hearing society.

"Picking up" Languages

All of the seven women who taught their children ASL also wanted their children to learn spoken English. Two spoke of reading stories in English while also signing to their children as a way of having their children simultaneously connect the two languages of English and ASL. This, then, is another aspect of the work where these mothers teach their children, as all mothers do, to communicate in a variety of ways. These deaf women, however, were also making decisions about their children and if they should be bilingual so that they might be a part of both the Deaf and hearing worlds. How the mothers chose to teach their children to communicate or how they labeled their children as deaf or hearing was often met by opposition from people in the Deaf community or from members of the hearing world. Part of the work of these mothers, then, was to resist this opposition in various contexts.

Stephanie's story illustrates how part of her work as a deaf mother has been to actively resist such labeling of her children as either hearing or deaf:

> S: Often people ask me if they are hearing or deaf. I tease them a little bit, "oh yes, this is Sara." They ask, "No, I mean are they hearing or

deaf?" I say, "This is Sara." They say, "What's wrong, don't you want to tell me?" Means hearing, deaf, not important. The children will pick it up. (She implies that hearing people told her she should speak to the children or they won't speak "well.") They will listen to the TV, radio, friends, family, relatives, friends (She makes a sign like "it's all there."). Hearing people have many ways of (She signs something that looks like "taking it all in.") So, that's why my husband from day when each child was born, we sign already.

Stephanie, by treating her three hearing children as individuals rather than as either abled or disabled, uses this as a strategy for negotiating her and her children's identities as deaf, hearing, or in between the two worlds. Her statement of how her children would "pick up" English echoes many of the deaf women's stories about how they themselves "picked up" ASL. The process of "picking up a language" is, of course, not unique to deaf or hearing people; rather it occurs and shifts in each family, school setting, and the other places where people develop languages. Her comments also show that spoken English is not a "natural" trait of hearing or deaf people as some, although not all, members of the medical community have proposed. Rather, these experiences suggest that language is something that is learned in various contexts and that one's primary language partially depends on where one learns language. Where and how one learns language became key factors for these women and their children as they made places for themselves in the deaf and hearing worlds.

Carol, who, unlike Stephanie, at first did not actively teach her hearing daughter sign language, discussed how she worried about when her daughter would learn sign language. After speaking with other deaf women who had hearing children, she realized that her daughter's process of developing language, both ASL and English, was quite "normal:"

Carol: They said you don't have to worry about it. She will pick it up later on, when they're older. 'Cause right now they're like (She shrugs her shoulders as if to say "indifferent."). So, I'm sure she'll pick up more signs. Sometimes if I don't understand her, I say "you have to sign." (She pretends to be her daughter and shrugs and rolls her eyes.) That age, you know. But right now, I try not to force her. I think eventually she will sign. I think right now she thinks "oh, I can talk." But then sometimes, I wear hearing aids. But sometimes I don't wear a hearing aid. But she, not realize it. "Mom, Mom." Then she (She taps the floor with her foot and waves her hand.). You know. (laughs) (She slaps her shoulder.) But I notice that she (She makes a sign for "eye contact" but does not

verbally say it.). Has to have that eye to eye contact. I mean, she wants
to get my attention. Because I have to look at her. Because I do that to
her (She pretends to tap me and get my attention.). It depends on the
mood. Sometimes we test my daughter, can you answer in signing?
"O.k." I want to make sure she understands. But, I don't want to force
her to sign. I want her to decide which way to learn more.

Despite her daughter not completely knowing sign, she is, as Carol
describes, gaining the skills of how to talk with someone who is deaf. As
Carol mentions, her daughter has learned to tap the floor or wave her hand
when her mother does not wear her hearing aids to get her mother's attention. Carol mentions how sometimes she and her husband will "test" her
daughter with sign language so that they can understand each other; however, she makes it clear that she wants her daughter to actively decide how
she will speak. One can see from this that another part of the work of
mothering is to empower one's children to make decisions about their languages so that they, as well as the women, may become active agents in
constructing their identities.

Hybridity and "Going Back and Forth"
All of the nine women who had more than one child talked about differences *among* their children with regard to learning languages. The ages of
the children and the number of children in a family were factors in how the
children learned languages. These stories relate to the experiences of the
women themselves when they were growing up and learning to "go back
and forth" between languages in the different contexts of families and
schools. Debbie, who taught her hearing husband sign language, also
described how they and their two hearing children communicate as a family in what she calls a "hybrid form of communication:"

D: Both the kids are a little bit different. The son. Well, both are easy
to lip read. Easier than my husband. My son will sign. My daughter is a little bit shy. And I've learned from talking to other people
that the second or the third child don't sign as much as the first.
Because the first one is talking to the second one. I'm trying now,
I'm trying to teach her. She knows some signs, but I like her (she
signs "more").

C: Are you trying to teach them ASL or English?

D: They're mix. I don't want to pressure them just because of me. It's
up to them. I want them to be themselves. There are some parents
I know who pressure them "you must sign. You must sign." Whatever they want. I remember with my son, I was worried if he

would be able to speak right because I don't speak right. So, I had tapes. Stories, songs. But he speaks very clearly. So, I don't worry about the second one. Because I knew he would talk to her. Plus they're a few years apart. I want him to be able to interact with hearing people. Not feeling different because of me. Not talk differently because of me. You know, not about me. So, it's what we call a hybrid form of communication.

Debbie, like Carol, wants her hearing children to play a role in how they will develop languages; however, she also describes how she actively works to teach them "appropriate" speech by having tapes where she would, along with the tapes, read stories and sing songs to the children. This work creates an environment where her children are learning how to go "back and forth" between the two languages of ASL and spoken English. Six of the seven mothers who had all hearing children mentioned that they didn't worry as much with their younger hearing children as they knew they would develop English by listening to their older siblings. The exception was Teresa who primarily used oral methods while communicating with her children, perhaps because of her strong oral upbringing as well as being the oldest woman in this study.

Stephanie also spoke of differences in how each of her three hearing children developed their languages. She describes how each of the children learned ASL, English, and the art of going back and forth:

C: So, all your kids sign.

S: Oh, yes. They all sign.

C: Would you say it's ASL?

S: Yes. O.k., all three are different. Sara, ASL. Very skilled. I believe it's her P-R-I-M-A-R-Y language. Her first language is ASL. Now she's good at both, going back and forth. Spoken English to ASL. Back and forth. She's good. The second, first language is English. (She is now referring to Maureen.)

C: When you say English, you mean English like me?

S: Yes. Spoken, not sign. Sign little. Because Sara would be with her talking and she would be talking to her and then signing to us. For example, Maureen and I were at the table signing, Sara didn't know that I was talking to Maureen because we were signing, no voice, she didn't know. (She pretends she is Sara.) "Maureen." Talking. Maureen would look at her. I would look at Maureen. "What about, where's Sara?" Oh, Sara is in the other room talking to Maureen. Maureen was looking at the sound. So, I went to the other room. (She pretends to talk to Sara.) "We were talking. (She pretends she is Sara.) "Oh, I didn't know." But, that's why Maureen's first language is spoken English because she learned from Sara. But, Maureen learned sign, yes. Since she was a baby. Also, she responded to sound first. Fine, I accept that, fine. (She points to her third finger to discuss Robbie.) Since we moved here, he was eleven months old. Sign. Sara went to school, afternoon and morning. Maureen went to nursery school. Robbie and I were together and he paid attention to my voice and signing. I believe his primary language is ASL. Up until now, Sara can go back and forth from English to ASL. Sara can talk with her voice, sign, ASL. Maureen can sign and speak at the same time. Shut her voice off, maybe, she like talking and signing at the same time. Voice, Maureen, can't shut off her voice. Robbie can't go back and forth. It has to be one or the other.

C: Oh, he can't switch.

S: Talking or shut off the voice signing. He can't go back and forth.

C: So, Robbie would you say is the most ASL?

S: When he was a baby he was ASL, yes. Later, he can do both, but he can't go back and forth.

C: He can't switch back like Sara.

S: Yes, because she was the first child. Fine, with the others would learn, but she would learn from us. If I'm older, I want them to sign. But, each child, their skills are different because of their experience. When I sign, it's different with everyone. Same as everyone. It reflects their personality. With hearing kids you can see their personalities. It's the same with people who have signing skills, you can see it.

Stephanie's comments illustrate how having multiple hearing children can influence how the family communicates as well as how the members might think of themselves as relating to the deaf or hearing worlds. Sara, the first born, since she was at home with her deaf mother and father, learned ASL as her primary language and then has learned how to go back and forth between ASL and English. Maureen, who would also learn ASL, uses her voice to communicate along with sign language. Finally, Robbie whose primary language is also ASL, struggles with going back and forth between the languages, perhaps because he was at home with his mother while his siblings were in school. The seemingly invisible work of this deaf mother plays a huge role in how these family members negotiate their identities and make decisions about belonging to the Deaf community, the hearing world, or somewhere in between. Stephanie's comments also show how she works to "normalize" these experiences as she comments that this process of learning languages is the "same" for both hearing and deaf individuals.

Heather, as with the other women, adds to our understanding of teaching one's children how to "go back and forth":

> H: I taught Brian signs like "milk," "eat." Basic signs. He signed (She makes a sign that looks like "growing up."), but starting two, three, he signed less, talk more. Because of daycare. At home I talked to him a lot. Should have signed too, but I didn't.

> C: Is he signing ASL or?

> E: English. He finger spells words. But as he got older, five, six, years old, I noticed he talked a lot more to me. And I didn't understand him most of the time. His lips are hard to read. Too small. I realized, his mother's deaf, his father's deaf and he didn't know much sign. So I decided to turn off my voice, turn off my hearing aids and sign to him. At first it was hard, but he picked it up very fast. I'm hoping that he'll sign more, but it did work, he did sign.

> C: And now is he signing ASL?

> H: No, English. It helps me with communication.

> C: And then what about with Jeffrey? The younger one.

> H: He's signed since he was a baby. He talked later than Brian. Because Brian take over the talking. Talks for him. Brian's more in the mind, you know. And Jeffrey's more physical. Jeffrey signs, half English, half ASL. And now he's five and he signs. Talks sometimes.

One can see from Heather's story that the process of teaching children to go back and forth is an ongoing process and also partially done by learning how to do this as the children grow up. Heather did not teach her oldest son to sign first and then, after he went to daycare and was speaking more, learned that she and her son struggled with communication between them. This then led to her not using her voice and signing to him. Heather, who grew up oral, used English grammatical order with the sign language. Of the nine women who grew up primarily oral, four spoke of sometimes using English grammatical order with the sign language, which suggests that growing up oral influenced how some of these women raised their children. Heather's second son, who she signed with since birth, is seemingly able to go back and forth more easily than his older brother. Her story also shows that the work of these deaf women is an ongoing process where part of the work is to investigate different strategies for teaching their children languages at various points in their lives. In this way, Heather was able to resist this obstacle of not being able to communicate as well with her hearing son after he learned more English from his hearing daycare environment.

"Going Back and Forth" Within the Deaf Community

Another skill, which all of the women taught their children, was the art of going back and forth with members of the Deaf community. For example, three of the women described instances where children were able to know if they should sign as well as speak to a particular deaf person. As mentioned earlier, Carol's daughter was able to know the differences of how to communicate with her mother when she wore or did not wear her hearing aids. Carol also mentioned how her hearing daughter knew the differences between other members of the Deaf community:

> Carol: She knows I have some friends who don't talk. She knows she has to sign. She knows she has to sign to that person. And then if someone talks like me over there, she can talk. It's been a good adjustment.
>
> C: So even *within* the Deaf community she knows some people it's o.k. sign, it's o.k. drop it. But certain deaf people you need to sign, she knows the difference.
>
> Carol: Yeah.

Carol's story illustrates another part of the work of these deaf mothers, which is to teach their children the subtle differences of communicating with members of the Deaf community. One result of this for the women and their families was that how they, as a family, related to members of the hearing and deaf worlds influenced how they identified themselves in these worlds. In this way, Carol's decision influenced her daughter's sense of herself as she was teaching her daughter the cultural differences of communicating with members of the Deaf community and working to ensure that her daughter was a part of this community as well as of the larger hearing society.

How will our extended families communicate?

All of the women talked about communicating with members of their extended families and how this worked and often changed with the births of their children. Their comments show that how their children learned ASL, English, and other ways of communicating influenced how each family related to members of their extended family. Three women spoke of hearing relatives learning sign language in an effort to communicate better with their family. Often, having their own families provided a space where these women changed how their own extended families thought of what it meant to be deaf, hearing, or in between. The women, in these instances, developed various strategies where they negotiated fuller participation in their extended families as part of their work as college educated deaf mothers.

Learning Sign

Although Ellen's father was not able to learn sign language while Ellen was growing up, due in part to his work demands, he is now learning sign language in an effort to communicate with his two deaf granddaughters. Ellen describes this, as well as how her older deaf brother reacted to her having deaf children:

> E: Now, my father a little bit learning sign because my daughters, two, are deaf. (smiling) Father, stuck. Has to sign a little bit. When I bring her to my parents to take care of her, my parents sign. (She points to Kate.)
>
> C: Now how did your [deaf] brother feel about that?
>
> E: Surprised. Happy. It's good for us.

Ellen's comments suggest that with the addition of her two deaf children, her birth family is changing how they communicate. She also mentions, as did Janice, the only other women in this study who had a deaf sibling and deaf children, how her deaf brother was happy about the addition to the family. One can see that, in these two cases, as more deaf people were born into these families, it influenced how the larger family groups not only interacted and communicated, but also how the women and their families negotiated their places in the deaf and hearing worlds. These women developed this as a strategy for integrating themselves and their families into their larger extended families.

Changing the Location of a Family Event: The Invisible Work of Sociability

Not all extended families learned sign as the women had their children. No woman in this study who had hearing children mentioned their extended families learning sign language, which shows that having deaf or hearing children greatly influenced how these families communicated. While the extended families of women who had hearing children might not have learned sign language, the women and these relatives used alternative strategies to communicate. Teresa, the mother of three hearing children and grandmother of three hearing grandchildren, described how she would sit next to her daughter's father-in-law at family functions and how they would each type back and forth on her computer as a way of communicating. Another strategy which one of the women spoke of was to change the location of a major family event. Carol's example of inviting her extended family to Thanksgiving at her house for the first time illustrates how this kind of work relates to negotiating her deaf identity:

> Carol: When we had Thanksgiving at my home. The family came. Oh, big difference. We always had Thanksgiving at our home growing up. No one would pay attention to us. I invited many to us. Focus on us, make sure we understand what's going on. We have a conversation. But, somebody else's home, different. (She shrugs her shoulders and laughs as if to say "we're lost."). I learned something. We're o.k. with small groups of people. My sister, her family, and us, we all, we're o.k. Big party (She shakes her head "no" and shrugs her shoulders.).

By having Thanksgiving at her home, Carol was able to create an environment where members of her extended family made more of an effort to ensure that she was included in the family conversations. As DeVault (1991) has argued, women often do the invisible work of sociability where they create "family" through the rituals of preparing, organizing, and having family meals. Changing the location of a family event along with the work of sociability are things that many women, hearing or deaf, do as a way to define themselves as well as their family groups. For Carol, this also became a way to resist her extended hearing family's usual oral way of communicating. Carol created a space for herself where she became a greater part of her extended family as well as negotiated her identity as a deaf woman in her larger family group. Her strategy of creating this space is another example of part of the work of mothering.

DECISIONS ABOUT CHILDREN'S EDUCATION

As with decisions about their children and communication, the women in this study also gave serious attention to how they would educate their children in both formal and informal contexts. For all of these women, decisions about ASL and English were important to these decisions. The women, and the three that had deaf children in particular, also advocated for their children in various contexts as well as taught their children be their own self-advocates and how to educate people about deafness. For three of the seven women who had hearing children, enrolling their children into Kids of Deaf Adults (KODA) camps where their children would interact with other children who had deaf parents became another strategy for educating their children as well as a space where these families negotiated being in the Deaf world, the hearing world, and in between the two.

Teaching them at Home

All of the women used the home as an informal classroom, as most mothers do, where they taught their children about communication. Ellen, who had not opted for a cochlear implant for her hard of hearing daughter, viewed speech therapy as a necessary part of her daughter's education and took her to these classes three times a week. Although these were formal lessons, Ellen also practiced speech at home with Kate when they read stories together aloud. Another place where Ellen tried to get Kate to practice her speech was on the phone with other relatives:

> E: I bring her to a woman for speech every week. Three times a week.
>
> C: So, you want her to talk plus sign.
>
> E: Yes. I want her to look at the signing and the speech and talk on the phone. Her Aunt. [who is hard of hearing]. (She pretends to be two people talking on the phone.) You know, know everything. I want her (She points to Kate as if to say "I want her to be like her Aunt.").

Ellen's strategy of educating her daughter about communication is to use a blending of methods, which include formal speech therapy lessons as well as informal lessons such as talking on the phone and reading stories. The work that Ellen does to ensure that her daughter picks up spoken English is part of the invisible work that all of these mothers do to actively negotiate what it means to be deaf, hearing, or a combination of both. This decision to use a blending of communication methods reflects how, although Ellen considers her and her family a part of the Deaf community, she also wants her daughter to be able to relate to the hearing world.

Another example of how these women taught their children at home is Kristen's story of teaching her two deaf children "cued speech," which she learned herself four years ago. She explains how her husband's, as well as her own experiences while growing up, have influenced their decisions about how to educate their own children about communication:

> K: I was thankful that I learned ASL because it enabled me to have two languages. English (She moves her hands apart.) ASL, two different. If I didn't learn ASL, I may struggle with English. Because I've seen so many people who grew up oral, some manage beautiful, but they couldn't fit in the Deaf world because they can't sign.

Because they're hearing. (The way she signs "hearing" is not the usual sign here at the mouth, but rather at the head as if to say that you think you are hearing.) But, deaf. Hearing people think they're deaf. But deaf people look at them, they're hearing. It was a battle for my husband. He grew up oral. He never met a deaf person, he never signed until he came to NTID when he was twenty-two years old. It was a culture shock for him. So, now we both agree, we have deaf kids. We're gonna teach them sign, lip read, speech reading, cued speech. We use that at home.

C: Cued speech. What is that?

K: Cued speech is a communication tool for eight handshakes that represent consonants, vowels. It helps you to identify things. So you can hear the [syllables that are not lip readable]. Deaf people can't hear them. They can see visual cue. For example, but, mut, put (She fingerspells the words.). This is "b" but, "m" this is m, put, this is "p" (She makes different movements with her hands.) They're cued. It's hard, but same with you, you learn sign language. I'm learning cued. My deaf kids will be able to pronounce clearly. The syllables. Right. This is "r" (She makes a movement with her hands.) Right. There's a "t" at the end. Right. That's right. (She makes the movement again coming from her throat.) Appropriate. Ap-pro-pri-ate. (She makes a different movement with her hand for each syllable, each one coming from her throat.) Ap-pro-pri-ate. Now, signing, "right," "appropriate," "typical" (She signs each of these words, which all have the same sign.) They look the same. Some deaf kids won't develop new vocabulary words to expand. So, cued speech helps them. It's not ASL (She signs something that looks like "that's separate.") I would say [it's a combination of] oral, speech reading, lip reading, and phonics.

By explaining how learning ASL as well as English has made her "able" to move more easily between the worlds of the deaf and the hearing, Kristen suggests that deafness is an asset rather than a "disability." By learning cued speech, in her opinion, her deaf children will be able to develop new English vocabulary words and pronounce words more clearly. Although various members of the Deaf community might see cued speech as a further attempt to colonize the Deaf, Kristen makes the decision to teach her children this method because, in her opinion, it will give her children an advantage in a larger hearing society. Kristen and her husband are both actively involved in the Deaf community in Rochester and consider themselves part of the larger Deaf community. Their example shows that they play an active role in negotiating their own deaf identities as well as those of their children. It also illustrates the responsibility placed on Kristen and her children in order to ensure the children's future educational success as well as to make decisions about their identities.

Other Ways of Teaching

Other areas where these women negotiated decisions about their children's educations were in the formal spaces of classrooms, at home with babysitters, and in their relationships with other mothers. The three women who had deaf children struggled with whether to send their children to public schools where they would be mainstreamed, private schools, or schools for the deaf. The seven women who had hearing children often struggled with communicating with their children at home after the children went to hearing schools. Features of the local community seemed to especially matter for the families and how the women were seen as mothers as well as how they were accepted by members of the Deaf community or the hearing world.

Hearing Children Learning Sign and Speech

Carol, who works at a manual state residential school for the deaf, enrolled her hearing daughter in the daycare at her work. This worked well for a time as it was both convenient and gave her daughter an opportunity to meet other hearing and deaf children who had deaf parents. Carol's daughter then went to public school where she was with all hearing children. Carol describes the shift and how this affected the family:

> Carol: She was signing when she was little. When she'd go to the daycare she's sign. Once she entered public school she (She signs "talked" but does not verbally say it.). It's fine. I accept that. That's her, I want to meet her needs. I didn't want her to meet my needs. I didn't want her to be stuck with me. I didn't want her to be like an interpreter for me all the time. Because I don't want to obligate her growing up. I want her to feel comfortable coming home. But, she signs when she feels like it. But it's interesting, when my husband and I sign, she understands.
>
> C: So she can see and understand it?
>
> Carol: Yeah, she tells my mother what we're talking about. Then we laugh. It's funny.

Although Carol's hearing daughter is now signing less because she is in a hearing school, she is able to understand ASL when her parents sign to each other. Carol, like four of the other women with hearing children, spoke of not wanting to "obligate" her daughter by forcing her to learn sign language.

Carol's strategy of letting her daughter make decisions about how she will communicate is an example of the work of these deaf mothers which involves empowering their hearing children to negotiate their own identities. Another strategy is to resist putting her hearing daughter in the position of being a translator for her in various settings.

Locations Matter

None of the Boston women spoke of location or their community making a difference in decisions about their children's education; however, all of the Rochester women spoke of the influences of the Deaf community on their mothering experiences. Of these women, Janice and Stephanie moved to Rochester after attending and working at Gallaudet University in Washington, D.C., where the Deaf community also differs from the one in Rochester. Janice describes this cultural shift when she and her family moved from D.C. to Rochester:

> J: What was it like when I lived in Washington, DC.? I had deaf friends. Deaf community, signing, was like "why are you sending your kids to public school?" Because my husband and I are both deaf. "Why not they go to school for the deaf?" We (She makes a sign like "pushed them aside.") said, "we're doing the best for our children." Not send them to deaf school because our children had a lot of hearing, so we decided what was the best for them. When we moved here, people here were more accepting of differences. More patient.

The changes in community influenced decisions that Janice and her husband made about their children's education. At the public school, her children would have services for the deaf, but would also be required to learn spoken English, which Janice saw as a necessary skill. Her story further shows that the work of mothering also involves making decisions about their children's formal educations, how they will learn language, and how they will relate to the Deaf community, the hearing world, and the spaces in between.

Stephanie's story shows another experience of a cultural shift after she and her family moved from D.C. to Rochester:

> S: It was good. It's good we lived here. It's nice. It's my home. It's a challenge. I miss my babysitter in DC. I had this babysitter in DC. She was great. She herself had a cochlear implant. She knew how to finger-spell. So, we could communicate well. That was good. I miss her. When I live with the children here, now, I appreciate that babysitter to teach my children.

Stephanie describes how she now misses her babysitter who had a cochlear implant because she used to sign with Stephanie as well as with the children. Perhaps due to location and a difference in Deaf communities, it has been harder for Stephanie to find someone in Rochester who she can communicate with to assist her with the work of mothering and teaching her children to be bilingual. Thus, changes in deaf communities influenced how these women did the work of mothering.

After her husband got a job transfer to work at NTID, Teresa, who did not know ASL, and her family moved from the Midwest to Rochester where she was exposed to the Deaf community for the first time:

> T: That was in 1975. This was another Deaf world for us. Strong Deaf culture. We didn't have that in [the Midwest]. So, many oral, so many manual, so many (She makes a noise with her mouth like "phttt" and spreads her hands around. I believe this is a sign in ASL and it means something like "spread out."). But here (She makes a circular movement on the table and brings her hands together.), close knit community. Sandy was five. Steve was ten. And Kimberly was nine. Pull roots for me. (She sighs and shakes her head.) Took me five years to adjust.

> C: Wow. Why?

> T: I just missed (She signs "communicating."). I was still (She signs "communicating" and appears to be struggling with it.) with communication. I was not fluent enough with my sign to be able to sit and talk (She makes a noise "phttt" and puts her hands out from her chest, another sign I believe is ASL.) with women friends. That was the culture shock I went through coming here from [the Midwest]. Career women. Me, housewife. It was too much. I'm not a career woman, I'm a woman at home. Where are the mothers? They're all working.

Teresa's description of "culture shock" echoes many of the women's educational experiences when they learned ASL for the first time, however, her culture shock involves her work of mothering. Since Teresa grew up oral and attended a hearing college, this was the first time she was exposed on a large scale to the Deaf community. This cultural shift affected how she was able to develop relationships with other mothers, not only because of challenges with language, but also because she was a stay-at-home mother. Teresa struggled with being a mother in this new location with a strong Deaf community, despite her deafness, because she identified more with being oral. One can see from her story that decisions about where they will live influence how these deaf mothers carve out places for themselves in the deaf world, hearing world, or places in between. The decision to live in a particular kind of Deaf community was yet another decision that many of these women and their families made, which was part of the work of mothering.

Teaching the Skills of Lifetime Educators and Self-Advocates to Deaf Children

Advocating for their children, and then later teaching them the skills of being self-advocates as well as lifetime educators, were strategies that all of the mothers developed in their motherwork. As discussed in chapter three, these learned skills were ones that the women developed through their experiences of advocating for their own educations. Part of the work of mothering was passing down these skills to their children, especially for the three women who had deaf children, so that they might more easily negotiate their way in a larger hearing society.

Mothering and Lifetime Educators

Stephanie, along with her hearing children, did the work of a lifetime educator to educate members of her children's schools about the Deaf community. Here she speaks about the work of being a mother and lifetime educator:

> S: My hearing children's experience is different from their hearing friends. Their children meet friends or at church say "can your mother speak?" (She pretends she is a friend of one of her kids.) Or "can you interpret for your mother?" I always make myself clear to my children, "you don't have to be my interpreter. Stay children. If they ask you, no, they write me or talk or point." I support them. I want to make sure they stay kids. Because I can be with them, they can learn to communicate with us (She is referring to her children's friends.). So, I support them and stay their mother role. Professor. I can say that because for a while I saw my children doing research. Small research. Small projects. Sweet children. They want to know about deafness. So, I sat with them. I can help them find information about deafness give it to them for their school projects or research. I'm really proud because I can teach them. They learn a lot about deafness. I feel I'm an educator. Mother role. Supporter.

Stephanie teaches her hearing children to educate their friends about her as a Deaf woman while also advocating for herself so that they will not be placed in the role of an interpreter. She also encourages her hearing children to advocate for themselves by educating their peers about the Deaf community. Stephanie also is a lifetime educator as she educates her children who become educators themselves to their hearing peers about the Deaf community. One can see, then, that part of the work of mothering is to pass down the skills of being a lifetime educator as well as a self-advocate to one's children.

Advocating for their Children

Kristen discusses how she left her job to ensure that her deaf children got the necessary services:

> K: I loved that job. At that time, I discovered my son was deaf. I realized that I want to channel my time and energy to make sure he gets all the services. Now my family, my role. I have different hats. I'm a mother, a teacher, I'm a mentor. I'm a facilitator. I'm a role model. My kids, I'm an educator. Advocate for them all the time. I go visit the school.
>
> C: Where do they go to school?
>
> K: [An elementary] hearing school. Total mainstreaming. They have interpreters. They have teacher of the deaf. They work with the regular teacher to make sure they're up to the par.
>
> C: Very different than your experience.
>
> K: Oh, yes. As my role as a mother, I believe, so important for both my kids with their deafness, they have to work three times harder to be close to hearing peers and not to use their deafness as an excuse (She holds up her pointer finger and shakes it at me.). (We both laugh.) "Yes, you're deaf. Accept. If you want to be someone, dream. Work hard."

Having had to advocate for herself at a young age, Kristen saw how necessary this would be for her children and knew the amount of work involved, which led her to quit her job. Janice and Ellen, the other two deaf women in this study with deaf children, also quit their jobs when their children were young to advocate for their educations. Of the seven women with hearing children in this study, four mentioned quitting paid jobs to stay-at-home with their children. These stories suggest that this places an unusual and unfair amount of work on the women, especially for those with deaf children, while they fight for their children's educations. None of the women in this study mentioned that their husbands quit their jobs to do the work of advocating for their children's educations, although they contributed to decisions about their children's educations. The work, then, is also gendered. Kristen's story above, further shows how part of this mothering work is to strike a balance between advocating for deaf children while also teaching them that they have a role in their own educational success.

Ellen, as part of her advocating work for her deaf children's education, also spoke about moving to a different community and state to ensure her children's academic success. Ellen and Peter mentioned that they were considering moving to Florida from Massachusetts because of their own experiences with the school system for the deaf in Massachusetts:

E: And (She points to Peter and the girls.) are thinking about moving to Florida. (She spells it "FLA.".). Maybe for her (She points to Kate.) and Emma's school. Education is very important.

C: What's in Florida? I don't know about the school there.

E: Florida has a deaf institution. Deaf and blind students there. Because we want a good education for her (She points at Kate.). Because here in Massachusetts, education is (She makes a sign where she shakes her hand as if to say "it's o.k.".). I prefer, we both do (She points to Peter.) to get education and to (It looks like she signs "advance.".). [The Massachusetts school system] for English, it stinks.

Ellen's example illustrates how the work of advocating for one's deaf child often involves making decisions about where one lives. Both Ellen and Peter want their deaf children to learn spoken English as well as sign so that they might learn English and get an education as a way of advancing themselves later in life. This work of mothering is done early, then, as Ellen's daughters are currently two years old and six weeks. Ellen and her family, who are somewhat economically comfortable, were hesitant to make the move because of the potential for financial risk. Kristen and Janice, the other two mothers who had deaf children and were economically comfortable, were able to move to Rochester where reputable schools for the deaf or programs for the deaf in public schools exist. This suggests that social class plays a role in how the women might be able to ensure equal access to educational opportunities for their deaf children and how they made decisions about their formal educations.

Finding One's Voice

Two of the three women who had deaf children told stories of how, after they had shown their deaf children the skills of self-advocacy and lifetime educating, the children developed these skills as they aged. Janice described when her entire family used these two skills at a YMCA camp that her deaf children attended:

J: My son and daughter are both advocates for themselves and help others understand. My children, one of their earliest experiences when they went to the YMCA camp. We asked for interpreters for them. We talked back and forth. They said they had a counselor who knew sign language. "O" (She pretends she is the counselor who was finger spelling and not signing ASL.) Basic finger spelling. One day, my son did not bring his baseball glove because he didn't know. A different counselor told all of the boys to bring their baseball gloves, but my son didn't know and he came home upset. We called a meeting with the administrator.

C: So, you and your husband, and your son?

J: Yes, and our daughter, our children.

C: Both the children?

J: Yes. They were ten and eight. We feel it was important for them to go in. That helped them to experience self-advocacy. My daughter asked the administrator "how would you feel if you were at an all deaf camp?" (She gives a look of shock that the administrator must have given.) So, they are really strong. I think we have raised them well.

Janice's story shows that these skills are learned and not natural to these deaf children as well as illustrates how Janice taught her children these necessary skills. These deaf children with mothers who consider deafness a linguistic minority rather than a disability and who teach these skills to their children are in some ways at an advantage over children whose parents might not adopt this philosophy as they negotiate their identities and places for themselves in larger hearing contexts.

Hearing Children attending KODA Camps

Three of the seven mothers who had hearing children sent their children to Kids of Deaf Adults (KODA) camps where they would meet and socially interact with other children who had deaf parents. These three mothers saw this as a critical piece to their children's education as sons and daughters of deaf parents. This work became another strategy of how these mothers, particularly those with hearing children, worked to resist their own stigmatized identities and having their children also be seen as different in larger hearing contexts. Stephanie described how her hearing son, who growing up played with her instead of his two older hearing sisters because they were already in school, went to a KODA camp:

S: He had to play with me. So we signed a lot in sign. But, then he grew, talking sign at same time, he can't. Because he knew English and ASL are different. Because he's a KODA. They went to camp. My son, first understand why he can't go back and forth. His skill. I think now he can go back and forth.

By attending KODA camp Stephanie's son was able to interact with other KODAs and better understand why he was not, at the time, able to more easily go back and forth from ASL to English. Stephanie described how this helped him to understand himself better and negotiate his identity as someone in between the worlds of the Deaf and the hearing. Her story shows that for the women who had hearing children, part of their work of mothering was to create spaces where their children could interact with people with similar experiences. The experience also improved communication between Stephanie and her son as well as with the other members of the family as he and they developed strategies for being in between worlds.

Carol, who also sent her daughter to a KODA camp, had a similar story:

> Carol: I like to see her get together with the other KODA kids. Because they can share things. Because they can share, "oh, same, same." Different than hearing friends, the parents different. Well, not really different. With the KODA they feel comfortable. They can talk, sign, they can do whatever. I like her to have both. The KODA group and the hearing friends. Even though I use an interpreter who is a CODA [Child of Deaf Adults who is over eighteen], I always ask them. So, they tell me their experiences and things like that. And she really looks up to older KODA kids. Like I have a friend who has two daughters. I asked them to baby sit her. I said, "you know those two girls, those sisters. Their parents, deaf." And she realized. "Oh, they're just like me. "Yeah. When you grow up you can be like them." She's "oh, cool." And now they have KODA camp.

Carol, by naming the two groups of her daughter's friends, "the KODA group" and "the hearing friends," despite the fact that the KODA friends are also hearing, suggests that there are important differences in the experiences of these two groups of children. Carol's comments also show that part of the work of deaf mothers with hearing children is to create environments where these children can go back and forth between these two worlds as they negotiate their identities as well as to resist having their children being seen as different in a larger hearing society.

Unpaid Work, Education, and Activism

Six of the women recounted experiences of how they, along with balancing their positions as mothers, also did activist work with the Deaf community. This included experiences with assisting other deaf individuals to get TTYs, teaching their children and their friends about deafness, and doing publicity for the Deaf community. The work of activism became a place where the women negotiated their identities as well as played a role in how they related to the Deaf world, hearing world, and the places in between these worlds. This work also involved making decisions about how the women saw themselves *within* the larger Deaf community.

The TTY Career

When pregnant with her first child in 1964, Teresa went with her husband to the New York World Fair where they saw a "picture phone" (which later led to the development of the TTY) on display at a phone company exhibition. After trying it out, they came home excited with the possibility of having a phone at home and contacted a friend who worked for Western Union. This friend got machines from a warehouse in California and connected Teresa's phone to her mother's home three blocks away, which made them the first people in the US to have such a phone. Teresa and Michael were then put in touch with another gentleman who had more machines. These events led to a volunteer TTY business which they ran out of their home:

> T: We started showing them to our friends. "I want one." (She shakes her head.) How, if you were all the way across town? Wire all the way (She pretends to be connecting a wire far away.) Impossible. We paid three dollars a month for that special hook up. Michael started investigating, using his electronics. We got all the teletypes and we installed them in deaf people's homes in [our city]. We were the first network because we had all of those machines. The man was great. He said, "you want these machines, you can have them." He put them in our garage and it was full of teletypes. Meanwhile, I had two children. Michael was going crazy. People would come and say "I want to buy one." I would say "o.k., give me the money." Then, Michael would go and hook it up. So, he was busy. All volunteer. Those years were the most important part of our lives. Then, Michael got an invitation at NTID, a job offer. But, he turned it down because he, two things, three things. He had a good job working at the new company. (She points to her second finger to show reason number two.). His wife was very pregnant with the third child. (She points to the third finger.) He was very deep in the work with the teletype.

By incorporating activism as part of her unpaid work, Teresa was also negotiating what it meant to be a working deaf mother. This work was so important to both her husband and her, that they chose to remain in the Midwest instead of moving to Rochester where there was a strong Deaf community so that they might improve the living situations of deaf people in the Midwest. Her story suggests that this unpaid work became a kind of career which was also closely related to how she navigated being in the Deaf world, the hearing world, and in between. It also shows how differences *within* the Deaf community affected how the women did their activism.

Teaching Children about Work as well as Deafness

Debbie describes how she takes her hearing children to the meetings of a nonprofit organization for the deaf to expose them not only to members of the Deaf community, but also to business culture:

> D: I'm on the board. Sometimes, I bring the kids to meetings. I have no babysitter. My son listens. It's a little bit above his head, but it gives him an experience. I told him, the meetings we talk about it's not all about being deaf. There are issues. Do we cut the program or do we start another program? This is business. (She pretends to ask her son.) "You think [this organization] is about deaf?" (She pretends to be her son.) "You talk about deaf, deaf, experiences at the meetings." (She pretends to talk to her son.) "No. We're talking about business, how to run the agency itself." I think that's important for the children to understand. I've wanted them to become involved in the non-profit sector. I saw my parents do that. They were very involved in many different kinds of organizations. They're the trustees of a school. My father's on the board for [an oral state residential school for the deaf] for twenty-five years.

Debbie, who sees learning about business from an early age as important and a way to gain access to success, wants to pass this skill on to her hearing children to ensure their future success. She uses her identity as a working mother and her identity as a deaf woman in her activist work while teaching her hearing children about business as well as about deafness.

Marie, who is the leader of her hearing daughter's Girl Scout Troop, also explained how the work of mothering is linked to her identity as a deaf woman in a nonprofit organization:

> M: It's my first year. I had no choice because nobody wanted to be the leader. A lot of mothers said "how can you do it with the four kids at home?" I said (She shrugs.) "I have no choice. I'll do it." So, I have eight girls. They were good about it. I have another mother helping me out. She can talk some of the time and I can talk some of the time. I get nervous because I'm not sure if they understood me or if they're (She looks around and rolls her eyes.). I say well, maybe that's typical of the

girls, just (She looks around.). Like if they find it boring or if it's just me they don't understand. I don't think they would stop me if they don't understand. That's why I'm glad to have the other mother help me out. They're thrilled to have me as a leader. But, I see one or two focus on the other mother who's helping me. But I have one or two that come to me. I feel good. But, I see more focus on her than on me. I think it's because of the communication lapse. Maybe they don't understand what I say all the time. I don't care at this point. If they feel comfortable with her, o.k. (She pushes her hands away as if to say "it's o.k.") If they feel comfortable with me, it's o.k.

Marie suggests that while doing the work of the Girl Scout Troop leader, she is also educating her daughter and her friends about deafness. As a role model for the girls, she is able to show her daughter and the Troop that she is able to do this job as part of her work as a mother. Like Debbie, this became a kind of invisible and often visible work which Marie did as part of being a deaf mother with hearing children.

Publicity for the Deaf Community

Other examples of activist work included getting publicity for the Deaf community by being part of organizations for the deaf, doing newsletters for Deaf organizations, participating in research regarding people with disabilities, or being on television. This activism was often done to educate others about the Deaf community as well as to advocate for themselves about their role as deaf mothers to both larger deaf and hearing audiences. Teresa, who also is the retired editor of a Deaf newsletter, founded a local advocacy group for Deaf women in Rochester:

> T: I was looking for some kind of (She signs "connection.") for me and my other deaf women. That was when there was more TV talk shows. Women were asking a lot of things about life. There was no captioning on television. And all the hearing people were "I learned this, I learned this." We were missing out on so much, so we were getting frustrated. So, [my friend] and I would talk about it. Learn more of how to function as full woman. We felt inadequate. While all of those hearing women were learning everything. We were still (She taps the table with both hands and looks around confused.) No relay service. No captioning on television. And so we formed Deaf Women of Rochester in 1981. There was a women's conference in New York City. What they were talking about on television. How to be assertive at the deaf conference.

How to handle working and mothering. We decided to give a workshop. Got very low response. (She gives a look of disappointment and surprise.). We ask around. I said, "wait a minute, there will be no hearing people there, just for us." "No research study?" That's what they were doing back then. So, deaf people were not interested. And so we got fifty women coming. And they learned, assertive. What's that word? We didn't know what that word meant. Speak up, if you don't like it, say something. We suffer, now we speak. "Can I bring my children?" No. "Can I bring my husband?" No. Only for deaf women. "Hearing friends?" No. Only for deaf women. We're just going to (She sits back in her chair as if to say "relax.") No children, running around, come back here (She pretends she is chasing kids.) Networking, learning, help.

Teresa's story shows that by doing this kind of activism where she was educating others about Deaf mothers as well as instrumental in getting other deaf mothers to advocate for themselves, that she also gained a stronger sense of herself as a Deaf woman. This not only influenced how she saw herself as a mother, but also influenced how she saw herself as a worker. Finally, it suggests that, by working to become a "full woman," her strategy of being an activist was one way that she resisted being stigmatized as different or perhaps incomplete by a larger hearing society.

Debbie, as part of her activist work and role as a working deaf mother, described how being involved in a federal study on women with disabilities was one space where she was able to publicly describe her experiences as a deaf working mother as well as to get assistance with her job search. All of the women in my study, by participating in my interviews, were also doing similar work as they each expressed a desire for people of a larger audience to understand their lives as deaf working mothers. Debbie describes her involvement in the other research project she participated in before I met her:

D: I was participating in the federal study. It's about women and disabled and jobs. I met this nice woman and I talked to her. Basically what they taught is resumes, networking. Now they're writing the report. They will send me the report in a year. I want to see what they have learned. There were some blind people. Some deaf women. There was MS. There was learning disability. Try and advocate. Really the underlying part, I feel, is self esteem. Self confidence. Be able to (She motions something like "go on.") They videotaped us so they hope to use us as an example for the rest of the nation.

Debbie's story of being involved in this federal research study is another example of how these women combined their work of mothering with activism as a way of negotiating their identities as deaf working women. By participating in this study and in mine, Debbie shows that she and the other women view this, in many ways, not only as an opportunity to advocate for themselves, but also as a way to educate people about deafness. In this way, her activist work was a place in which she developed strategies to educate a larger hearing audience about her deafness.

CONCLUSION

This chapter has uncovered the invisible work of deaf women concerning their children and communication and decisions about their children's formal and informal educations. In each of their stories, learning ASL and English became critical decisions regarding how these women did this work, which influenced how they defined themselves as mothers, workers, and as members of the Deaf world, hearing world, or the places in between. The learned skills of self-advocating and educating others about deafness, which were passed on to both their deaf and hearing children, suggest that the children as well as the mothers also became active agents in this ongoing process of negotiating one's identity in these worlds.

Findings for this chapter include making visible the various kinds of work that these deaf women did in developing their identities. They did this work by integrating themselves into their larger extended hearing families and their Deaf and hearing communities. Another type of work was to make political decisions about the languages of themselves as well as of their children. This resonates with literature by women of color who discuss the importance of language choices and the politics of racial and cultural difference (Anzaldua, 1990; Collins, 2000). The decisions of these deaf women about language are political ones because in making decisions about speaking English, ASL, or a combination of both, they carved out places for themselves and their families. If they raised their children to speak ASL, they and their families were seen as part of the Deaf community, whereas if they taught them spoken English, they were seen as more a part of the hearing world. The larger Deaf community and hearing society played a role in how these families were seen in regards to these cultural identities, but the women themselves also identified their decisions as political ones.

For example, Janice stated that she considered her and her Deaf family part of a larger "linguistic minority" and that they saw deafness as "cultural" rather than as a disability. By naming herself in this way and by her decision to teach her children ASL despite being part of a larger hearing society, she navigated the politics of her own as well as her family's cultural identity. Also, when the women of this study were asked how they identified themselves as Deaf, deaf, or hard of hearing, all, except for Heather, identified as Deaf or part of a group who considers themselves a linguistic or ethnic minority (Lane, 1999; Padden & Humphries, 1988). Despite not identifying as Deaf, Heather did describe being a part of the Deaf community. All of the women in this study, then, made similar political decisions about their identities as part of a linguistic minority. The three major ways in which these women made political decisions about their and their family's identities as Deaf included how they communicated in their personal relationships and families, communicated with their children, how they educated their children both formally and at home, which influenced how they saw themselves *within* the Deaf community.

Another finding of this chapter is that these deaf women developed three major strategies in defining themselves and their families. These strategies included "normalizing" their experiences as deaf mothers as not necessarily different from hearing mothers, recognizing various obstacles put before them as deaf mothers and working to resist these challenges, and incorporating activism in their unpaid lives to define themselves as deaf mothers. An example of where these deaf mothers resisted obstacles put before them is how they did the work of challenging their stigmatized identities in a larger hearing society. To do this work, they, through their everyday lives and experiences, voiced how they did not want their hearing children to be interpreters for them. This connects with scholars who have studied immigrant parents and how they are often put in similar positions where their children, whose native language is English, act as interpreters for them (Buriel, et. al., 1998). As with these immigrant families, the deaf mothers of this study were doing the political work of negotiating their identities as part of a larger linguistic, ethnic, or cultural minority.

Another way that the women in this study resisted obstacles put before them which would stigmatize their hearing children as different was to send their children to KODA camps where they could identify with others who had similar experiences. These findings also relate to scholars who study families with "disabilities" and how they often work to "normalize" their experiences (Harris, 2003; Traustadottir, 1992). The women of this study, then, as with these families, through the process of their everyday activities did the work of integrating themselves into a larger hearing society and resisted being seen as different.

Many of the women resisted various obstacles and challenges that were also put before them in their mothering and current paid work experiences. It is in these moments where we begin to see how the women, as well as their families, continually negotiate what it means to be part of the worlds of both the Deaf and the hearing, which influences the women's paid work experiences and opportunities. These experiences and the work involved, as described to me by many of the women, as being in "between worlds," is the topic of the next chapter.

Chapter Five
"Between Worlds:" Communication in Relationships and Paid Work Experiences

All of the women spoke of being in between the worlds of the Deaf and the hearing in their educational, family, and work experiences. How they learned American Sign Language (ASL) and English in their schools and families and used them to communicate in their workplaces influenced how they saw themselves as deaf women inside, outside, or between these worlds. The work of learning the languages of both worlds and their skills of knowing how to go back and forth between them affected their career experiences and opportunities. Many of the women viewed being bilingual as an advantage, as the sooner they acquired this skill the easier it was to negotiate their way in these two worlds. Being bilingual, however, influenced their social networks and educational experiences, which shaped where the women made places for themselves. This, then, affected their paid work environments and opportunities, sometimes limiting their opportunities.

This chapter has three sections which include how the women saw themselves "between worlds," their experiences of being in between worlds in their paid work experiences, and their experiences of balancing their mothering, paid work, and activism. Being in between worlds connects with the stories of their family, educational, and mothering experiences and affected not only what these women did for work, but also how they came to see themselves as deaf. While resonating strongly with the Deaf community and Deaf culture, due to the larger hearing society in their work, school, and family groups, they often worked to ensure greater ease of communication with both worlds. To do this, as was shown in Chapter

Four, the women made political decisions about their identities as Deaf women when they used their native language of ASL versus using English in various spaces. In most cases, if they used ASL, they were seen as Deaf whereas if they used English they were seen as deaf.

As seen in Chapter Three, making political decisions about their personal relationships, especially with their husbands and in their friendships, became part of the work of negotiating between two worlds. Their stories show that marrying deaf men and having deaf friends was often perceived as a political decision by others about whether they were a part of the Deaf community or hearing world. The women also actively resisted ideas of deafness as a "disability" and did things to show how they were instead part of a linguistic minority. They also developed strategies to ensure that their hearing children were a part of the hearing world. Teaching, for many of these women, became a place where they did the work of lifetime educating people about deafness and where they also resisted stereotypes that deaf people cannot teach. Those who worked in hearing offices developed strategies to integrate themselves into these kinds of environments. These included being lifetime educators, self-advocates, volunteering in these offices to prove that they were valuable employees, involving hearing relatives in "self-advocacy," and often denying a part of their own Deaf identity. Finally, the ways in which the women balanced their mothering, paid work, and activism connect with their experiences of being "between worlds."

"BETWEEN WORLDS"

An underlying issue of this study is the question of how to conceptualize "difference" in the everyday lives of these deaf women. Feminist scholars have written extensively about the politics of difference and the importance of balancing the risk of othering people along with making visible what, to some, might be groups of women about who little is known (Ahmed, 2000; DeVault, 1999; Maynard, 2001; Weedon, 1999). Labeling these women's experiences in the Deaf and hearing worlds, as I and they have done, is an attempt to organize their experiences by making them visible; however, this is a false divide. The women's experiences in these two worlds, of course, overlapped and there were also differences *within* these working environments and experiences. In an effort to analyze their lives in a social and political context, I have decided, in an effort to both organize and ground their stories, to use the language of these women, especially with regards to how they name being a part of the "Deaf world," "hearing world," or in "between worlds."

Teresa described what it meant to be part of the worlds of the Deaf and the hearing and how the experiences of family, school, and work all relate to being in "between worlds:"

> T: My experience is mostly working with deaf people. That is easy. Hearing communities can make an impact for deaf women in their jobs and their relationships. I'm in the hearing world a lot when it comes to working. My advantage was I could speak and lip read. I'm not the average deaf woman. I know a mother who, got married. She worked for many years in the hearing industry. Then, she was offered a job teaching at NTID. So, she's had the experience of working in both worlds. She said there was a BIG difference. She enjoyed the work with the hearing, but the socialization which is very important for a deaf woman's self esteem. She didn't have that coffee hour time, easy to be with people. One to one fine, but when they get together as a group, they suffer from that. So, getting together with a group of deaf women is "oh, relax," feel good about yourself and that can influence your children. I am in the hearing world with hearing friends, mother, father, grandparents. My children are hearing. The only deaf contact I have is my husband and work at NTID. So, it balances. Not many deaf women have that. Because I moved here when my children were a bit older, they were already established in a communication with me. I lip read with them. They did not sign. When we moved here, had more contact with deaf families, and that's when I saw for the first time, deaf mother and father with hearing children and sign was the major way to communicate at home. That wasn't the way I grew up.

A community can have an effect on the life experiences of a deaf woman in terms of her mothering and paid work experiences. Because Teresa was raised in a strong oral community in the Midwest, she raised her three hearing children to use English as their native language instead of learning sign. After moving to Rochester and experiencing a cultural shift, she redefined what it meant to be a deaf woman by becoming active in and working with members of the Deaf community. Later, this would influence her desire to work in the deaf world at NTID. Through her teaching and activism, Teresa integrated herself within the larger Deaf community where she learned ASL and developed friendships with other Deaf mothers.

Teresa's comments show some of the connections which exist between paid and unpaid work and how they shape the women's sense of themselves as deaf. She describes her friend, who struggled to make social connections at work, and how those kinds of experiences can, as she described, "influence your children" or how one defines being a deaf mother. These kinds of social relationships in the workplace become even more critical for these deaf women when they work in all hearing offices. Although Teresa considered herself as "not the average deaf woman," all of the other women in this study shared similar experiences of being in between worlds. Learning how to be a part of these two worlds is part of the work of these bilingual women. The stories in this chapter further illustrate the connections between paid and unpaid work as well as show the influences of personal relationships on these deaf women's paid work opportunities and experiences and their work as activists.

PAID WORK EXPERIENCES

This section describes how being in between worlds affected the paid work experiences and opportunities of these deaf women. There is a relationship between the paid work experiences of these women and how they went back and forth between worlds in their family and educational experiences. This section will describe experiences the women had as teachers, working in the hearing world, and working in a predominantly Deaf environment. It will uncover the work that they do in these environments to integrate themselves into their larger communities.

Experiences as Teachers

Eight of the ten women in this study had worked as teachers in residential schools for the deaf, colleges for the deaf, or in deaf education programs in hearing schools. Of these eight, four also taught and continue teaching ASL courses as either part of their current positions or as a part-time job. Six of these eight women still continue to work as teachers in their current positions or as an aspect of their job. The two exceptions are Teresa, who recently retired from her teaching position and Heather, who, although she works at a hearing university, is now a statistics analyst and programmer. Despite never having taught, Debbie and Marie have both worked at an organization for the Deaf, and Debbie continues to work there. Marie also worked as a Resident Advisor at NTID. Working in the deaf world, especially in a teaching capacity, is a common experience of these deaf women. All five of the Rochester women then have worked as teachers involved in deaf education while three of the Boston women have had these experiences. All of the women in this study have at one time worked for a school for the deaf or a deaf organization, and these kinds of work were important to how the women thought of themselves as deaf women. They often used their work as teachers to work as "lifetime educators" where they educated people about the Deaf community as well as furthered their own ideas about this community.

Although these women were often not seen as "legitimate" teachers in hearing schools or in oral state residential schools for the deaf, as I will show in the stories below, they were seen as able to work as teachers, tutors, and education administrators in deaf education programs. While the women negotiated spaces for themselves as deaf women, the places where they taught became sites where they identified with the deaf world, hearing world, or somewhere in between.

"Deaf people can't teach"

Teresa described her first work experience as a "teacher" at the oral state residential school for the deaf that she had attended earlier as a student:

> T: At that time [1960], women did not have a career. You became a teacher or a minister's wife. That was my college try. I'm not gonna marry a minister. Me, become a teacher? I can't be a teacher. Deaf people are not teachers. Deaf people can't teach. (She makes a movement toward me and then points to herself as if to say that we both know better.). I came home and I went to visit my deaf elementary school. Talked with the principal. She gave me a job there, teaching Home Economics and Gym. I was the first deaf teacher at that school. It was a total oral school. All the teachers teach speech and communication. I couldn't do that, so I never really had a real classroom. I could teach gym or home ec after school. That was my "teaching" (She puts her hands up and puts quotes over the word "teaching."). No sign. Talk, talk, talk, talk. I knew some signs then, but I couldn't use them. Very strong oral school. Still is today. It has become a cochlear implant school. All the kids have cochlear implants.

Due to her deafness, Teresa was not seen as able to teach, an occupation, in most cases, that is usually seen as women's work. As a former graduate of this oral school and a college educated deaf woman, however, she was seen as able to teach deaf children particular topics. Due to the philosophy of the school as well as the time in history, Teresa, who is at age sixty-three the oldest woman in this study, taught her students in the oral tradition. By describing the school today as a "cochlear implant school," Teresa shows that while ideas of deafness may have changed somewhat, that oralism still remains a strong aspect of deaf education programs and contributes to ways of thinking about what it means to be deaf. Through her paid work, Teresa was also defining what it meant to be a deaf woman. Thus, a strategy that she used in

developing her identity as a deaf woman was to resist becoming a "minister's wife" and instead work for pay as a teacher at this school. By working
for pay and marrying later in life, Teresa resisted what a larger hearing society might expect of her as a college educated woman who was also deaf in
the 1960s.

Getting into Teaching

As larger cultural ideas about deafness and deaf education underwent some
changes, Teresa, as well as the seven other deaf women, got positions as
teachers. No woman in this study, however, worked as a teacher at an all
hearing school. Although these deaf women got jobs as teachers and some,
for a short time, worked with hearing as well as deaf students, they all
worked with deaf students. While ideas may have shifted somewhat about
deaf women as capable teachers, those who do become teachers continue to
be tracked into work environments in the deaf world or working with deaf
students in predominantly hearing settings. Still, by working as teachers,
many of these women were the first generation of college educated deaf
women to work for pay. In this way, they were able to resist some of the
stereotypes of a larger hearing society that they were "unable" to work.

Beth's story illustrates how she made the shift from working in an all
hearing work environment to work at NTID:

> B: At my hometown in [the Midwest], I really faced a lot of discrimina-
> tion. People telling me that I was deaf. I couldn't do this. I wouldn't be
> able to answer the phone. And I thought that maybe I'd try here in
> Rochester 'cause they would know more about deaf people and they
> wouldn't be as discriminatory. But I was so wrong. The discrimination
> was still here as well. People would say, "well how are you and I going
> to communicate?" And I said, "it will be fine and just kind of work it
> out with me." And they would be like, "I don't know. What if the com-
> munication breaks down?" And I said, "just try me out and see." And
> they said, "well maybe we'll put you in the darkroom because there's
> not a lot of communication there." So, I was working in the darkroom.
> There wasn't a lot of creativity involved. It was more like I was doing
> typesetting for the printing. It was very boring, very limited. I had no
> communication with anybody. I just didn't like it so I began looking for
> a different job. My husband suggested, "why don't you look at
> NTID?" Because he never forgot that every time I arrived home from
> work I was starved for communication. I thought, "oh, o.k., that might
> not be a bad idea." And I did find a job at NTID working as a graphic
> designer working with the faculty and the staff.

After working in the hearing world as a graphic designer in two different geographical locations, Beth explains why she makes the decision to work in the Deaf world. As she mentions, she was put to work in a darkroom where little communication was involved or even could be as her native language of ASL is a visual one and the conditions of a darkroom would hinder such communications. In her new position at NTID, she was able to be in an environment where communication came with greater ease causing her to enjoy her work. Her relationship with her hard of hearing husband who also works at NTID shows that her personal connection with him led her to work in a similar environment in the Deaf world. Therefore, Beth's decision to pursue this job came in part from a decision to be part of the Deaf community.

Of the ten women in this study and the seven who had worked specifically at schools and colleges for the deaf, six of their husbands also worked in such places. Of these six, five of these husbands worked at the same school or college for the deaf as their wives. Currently, Beth and Carol's husbands still work at the same school for the deaf where the women are also employed. Debbie, Heather, and Marie, the three women who currently work in the hearing world, also seem to have a connection between their working environments and their personal contacts. Debbie's husband is hearing, Heather is divorced, and Marie's husband is hard of hearing and both she and he work for her father-in-law's family business. The relationships that these deaf women developed with their husbands illustrate that they used and in some ways needed these personal contacts and networks in order to get jobs.

Beth's career path continued at NTID where she was asked, through the connections that she developed with faculty in her job and in her part-time Master's program, to teach an ASL course. Currently, she is in a tenure track position at NTID as an Assistant Professor. After her unsatisfying experiences in the hearing work environment, Beth then sought employment in the deaf world where she was encouraged to pursue a career where she also teaches ASL. Due to the working environment and her identity as a Deaf woman whose native language was ASL, she was seen as "able" to teach; however, her story illustrates how these women can often be tracked into such professions because of their identities as college educated deaf women. Still, Beth's work as a college professor was a place where she resisted stereotypes from a larger hearing society that deaf women could not teach.

Working in the Hearing World

All of the women, except for Janice, had at one time worked in the hearing world. Of these nine women, seven had held professional jobs in the hearing world, whereas the other two, Kristen and Teresa, had worked part-time jobs in high school or college. Each of these nine women had stories of sometimes feeling socially isolated in their all hearing work environments. Four of the seven women who held professional jobs in the hearing world said that the feelings of social isolation were a major reason for leaving their job and taking a position in the deaf world. Of the three women who worked in the hearing world and developed social connections with their work colleagues which made them stay in these jobs, Heather is the only one who currently still works for pay in the hearing world. The other two women, Debbie and Marie, both volunteer part-time in hearing workplaces. Heather, however, as described earlier, has a job as a statistics analyst and programmer where she has little personal interaction with her hearing colleagues. How these women thought of themselves and the social connections that they did or did not make at work affected their employment opportunities. Heather, as I will describe later in this chapter, sought a job where little communication would be involved. Her current position allows her flexibility to sometimes work from home as well as to rely on email to communicate with her boss. Whereas this might cause some to feel socially isolated, Heather saw this as a benefit to her position as she less often struggled to follow along in office conversations. Although this situation worked for Heather, her story also shows how working in the hearing world often required women who were willing to have little social interaction with their colleagues.

"Lifetime Educators" in Hearing Workplaces

Stephanie's story shows how being a "lifetime educator" eventually prompted her to pursue other work opportunities in the Deaf world:

> S: With the Deaf community, I see everything. Talking-they would put the responsibility to me. In the hearing community, we have responsibility, yes. If they don't talk to me, I have to tap them and interrupt them, teach them what deafness is all about. I have to teach them some signs, if they want to learn sign. It puts the responsibility on me. Two way communication back and forth. That's what I really want. I don't mind teaching them. I envision myself as a lifetime educator. All my life I'm a teacher. To my children, to my parents, to hearing people. I'm always a teacher because I feel they learn from the deaf. I'm not angry for them, who not sign. That's normal. If you want to learn, I'm happy to teach you. If you want to communicate, I'm happy to work together. But, at the same time, I want them to teach me. Exchange. That's why I left the insurance company. I was fine. I had a lot of hearing friends. But, I feel I belong in the Deaf world.

Stephanie's assertion that she belongs in the "Deaf world," shows that because she, in this hearing workplace, had to do the majority of the work in order to communicate with her colleagues, that she came to identify more with the Deaf community and sought employment in the Deaf world. Since her colleagues did not know ASL, she offered to teach them; however, this was not an equal exchange. Although she had developed social relationships with her hearing colleagues, Stephanie did not feel she belonged in this hearing workplace, in part, because attempts to communicate were seen as her responsibility. Her strategy then to be seen as a "legitimate" and "successful" worker was to work in the deaf world where she could more easily develop the necessary social relationships and be satisfied with her job.

Feelings of Isolation

As stated earlier, all nine of the women that worked in hearing workplaces expressed having some feelings of social isolation in these settings. Carol, for example, described her experience of working in an all hearing electric company:

> Carol: They all talked. Sitting and talk, talk, talk, talk. I can't keep up with the conversation. I'm sitting and (She leans over like she's trying to understand them.). But, the problem is they're facing this way (She motions that they're facing away from her.). I need to lip read. I mean they were nice people. When they laugh, I don't know what they're laughing about. Once, I was at the [oral state residential school for the deaf where I now work], I was like (She pushes her hands away as if to say "forget it."). I mean, I can work with them. Hearing people. It depends who. They'd have a lunch break at like 12:00. So, we'd all have to go to the cafeteria. But, I don't really (She makes a sign that looks like "no one to talk to.") Then, I'd go back to work.

Because Carol's primary language differed from the "norm" in this hearing context, she struggled to make the necessary social connections at work, which influenced her overall satisfaction with her job. Once she began working at the oral state residential school for the deaf where she currently works, however, she felt more comfortable in her working environment where there was a mix of deaf and hearing people who were familiar with the Deaf community and some who knew ASL. Having an office environment where they can use their native language, greatly affects the career opportunities of these deaf women. Her story is also another example of how, by deciding to work in the Deaf world as a strategy, she was able to achieve satisfaction with her job, which is, of course, seen as part of how we measure "success." Despite being happy with her job, her story also shows how her opportunities to work in the hearing world were limited.

Doing the Work of Self-Advocacy and Resistance

Three women, Heather, Debbie, and Marie, who all had professional jobs in the hearing world, expressed enjoying their experiences in these positions. The women developed various strategies in their paid work experiences including where they self-advocated to ensure equal access in their working environments, resisted employer's unwillingness to make the necessary accommodations for their deafness, and resisted stereotypical notions of what it meant to be deaf. Marie illustrates some of these strategies:

> M: I feel the company itself is not people oriented. They think of themselves. I've request for interpreter, I've request for a TTY, I've request for everything, but they keep saying "no, no, no."
>
> C: Even with ADA [Americans with Disabilities Act]?
>
> M: Well, I explain about that. I said to myself, I knew I was gonna leave the company, I don't want to be put in that spot right now. I need that job. It's my first real job. So, I don't want to ruin it. My manager tried to support me. She tried to fight to get a TTY, but she couldn't do it either. The president of the company, they say "no." Working with the girls, the office, is great. I LOVED it. (She signs "interacting.") I keep in touch with them today. They realized that I could communicate well. They realized that I could do a good job. That I could joke around a little bit. So, they (She signs "interested.") They enjoyed being with me.

Although Marie was socially integrated in her first job outside of college, since she was not given the necessary accommodations to ensure her equal access in this working environment, she decided to look for other employment. As described in the educational histories in chapter three, many of these women knew when to self-advocate as well as when to hold back for what they needed in their work environments. Since this was Marie's first official job after college, she decided that it would not be in her best interest to fight for her rights as a deaf woman. Unless accommodations are made at the institutional level, then, these deaf women might not always be able to "succeed" in their work.

Finding a workplace where one felt socially connected as well as one that made accommodations for deafness was often hard and this limited the career opportunities of these deaf women. Knowing that finding an office in the hearing world that had both of these components was tough, many of the women, such as Marie, developed strategies to keep their jobs and climb the corporate ladder. In this way, we might imagine Marie's decision to stay at her job as a type of resistance to hearing employers who did not acknowledge her needs as a deaf employee; however, this is not to suggest that her career opportunities were not affected and limited by these experiences.

Another example of resistance to a hearing employer who was unwilling to make necessary accommodations for her deafness was Debbie's story:

> D: That was one of the best careers I have had because the team was small. I was able to grow within the team. And people understood my deafness and what my needs are. What was more challenging was that we serviced an outside class and we used a lot of email to communicate and video conferencing. When I rose up, it got to a point where I was participating in the video conferencing. My boss did not want to pay for the interpreter every week. So, instead, I asked a secretary to come to the meeting with a laptop and she'd type up the major words that were being spoken in the video. I could see the people, (She pretends to look at a screen.) video conference. I know who's speaking. And they could see all of us. The secretary would type and I would say something and then (She makes a sign like "it would go back and forth."). That worked out very well. I was still disappointed that my boss didn't want to have a real life interpreter, but I did want to keep my job, so I had to decide. That was so important to me. To be involved in the decision making. Many decisions would be made at that conference.

Debbie, struggling to get this job after getting her MBA, used a variety of strategies to ensure more equal access for her in this all hearing office. By seeking employment in a small office staff, such as she did by attending a small hearing college, she was able to self-advocate and educate members of her management team about her needs as a deaf worker. After her boss denied her the right to an interpreter, because she wanted to keep her job and saw it as a way to move up in her career, Debbie developed a strategy of having a secretary come and type up the video conference. This strategy was a way for her to resist being denied accommodations for her deafness; however, as with Marie, it did not give her complete equal access as not all of the conversation was interpreted. This experience then limited her career opportunities as a deaf woman. Also, as Debbie did not push to have the video conference be translated into ASL, she was, in some ways, denying a part of herself as a Deaf woman. For these deaf women to succeed in hearing workplaces, they were often faced with making political decisions about their identities as deaf women. As Debbie's story shows, one strategy often became partially denying being Deaf and a native ASL speaker in order to work in hearing offices.

Involving Hearing Family Members in the Work of Self-Advocacy and Resistance

Another strategy of these deaf women was sometimes to involve hearing family members in their self-advocacy and resistance to employers who were unwilling to make accommodations for their deafness. Four of the ten women in this study had stories of how hearing family members worked with them to negotiate situations in their paid work experiences. By having a hearing family member participate in such a strategy, these women were working to define who they were as deaf women. Often, by having a hearing family member come in to interpret, they were, in part, denying their Deaf identities as their hearing family members did not sign ASL. Thus, this method of translation was less than ideal. Ellen's story is an example of this kind of work:

> E: I worked there for four years. All the people working were hearing. I was the only one who was deaf. And my friends knew sign. Got involved with the sign. And they helped me interpret. For union meetings. I was involved in softball. It was hard to communicate with other people. Usually my sister would come and interpret. And I was not happy later with my friends. Because they a lot depend on me. Because I'm a good worker there. Hard. I can't hear them talking when working. I'm focused. I'm working, working, working. (She puts her head down and pretends that she is working on an assembly line.) hey depend on me more and more, so I quit. Five years later.

In her job at a clothing factory with all hearing people, Ellen shows that her hearing sister, by usually interpreting the union meetings, in some ways helped Ellen to socially integrate herself with her colleagues as well as resist the obstacle put before her by her hearing employer who did not make accommodations for her deafness by hiring a professional ASL interpreter. This strategy worked for a time until later her relationship with her colleagues changed as she felt that they took advantage of her as a hard working employee. As she describes, her colleagues would talk in spoken English while they were working, which led to Ellen being left out of the conversation and immersing herself in her work. Although having a hearing family member interpret worked for a time as a strategy for obtaining equal access at work, it did not provide the same kinds of equal opportunities that accommodations for deafness might allow these women. For these deaf women to succeed in an all hearing work environment, they needed to have accommodations for their deafness in place as well as establish social connections with colleagues.

Heather described how her mother helped her to negotiate the acceptance of a job in an all hearing office. Since the employer did not call on a TTY and Heather is unable to use the phone, she describes how her mom assisted her in accepting this position. She said, "My mother came up to my room 'you got the job offer.' (She pretends she is herself reacting to the news.) 'Oh!' I had to call them back whether to accept or not. Wait until the next day. The next day my mother called for me. She said I could start next week."

Heather's story, similar to Ellen's, illustrates how the women sometimes used the help of hearing family members as a strategy of self-advocacy to ensure access in or to hearing working environments. At the time, Heather was pregnant and both she and her husband, who were living with her parents, needed to find work. Since she wanted to make her transition to a hearing office as smooth as possible, she had her hearing mother assist her in negotiating the job offer over the phone instead of advising the employer to call her on a TTY. By doing so, Heather's strategy was, in some ways, an act of resistance to an employer who might have been unaware or perhaps unwilling to call by TTY because she wanted to ensure that she got the job. However, by having her hearing mother negotiate the job offer for her, Heather was also, in some ways, accepting a mode of communication that was less than ideal. Since Heather is the only woman in this study who currently works in the hearing world, her story, similar to Debbie's, shows that in order to work in the hearing world, deaf women have to, in some ways, be willing to deny their identity as Deaf women as a strategy for getting and keeping these jobs.

Volunteering as Another Strategy of Resistance: "I am deaf, but . . ."

Debbie, one of the three mothers who held a professional position in a hearing office and developed social relationships with colleagues, was recently laid off. Since she is currently a stay-at-home mother, she wanted to ensure a smooth transition when she does go back to working full-time. Volunteering at a hearing office, for Debbie, has become a strategy that she used to ensure later access to working in a hearing office:

> D: To keep my hand in business, I've been volunteering for a consulting company. I know I can put something on my resume because I know

that I'll be out of work for a long time. I have to convince people, I am deaf, but I'm o.k. I can work. I've got something in my mind. It involves a lot of communication and a lot of writing. I don't like to write. I'm sure a lot of deaf people have told you, they hate to write. I've learned that I have to challenge myself. Just do it. I go through more drafts than an average hearing person would do. For this volunteer, it's a little bit different than my previous job. It's an area that I'd like to test. If it's something that I want to change my career. If there's nothing there, I'll go back to what I've been doing. So, I have a backup plan. I've learned that I have to self advocate myself and tell people what I need. "I'm deaf. You don't write on the blackboard." (She pretends to do this with her back to me.) "You need to face me." When I need an interpreter, if I'm going to go to a class, who pays for it and so on. And work harder than my peers just to show who I am. That's what I've learned from working. They're cruel out there. But, I've learned to stay positive. I learn from mistakes.

One of Debbie's strategies is that she continues to work outside the home so that she can show future employers that she is knowledgeable in her field and would be an asset to their company. Her strategy is to dispel possible stereotypes of future employers of what it means to be a stay-at-home mother as well as what it means to be deaf. Another strategy that Debbie uses is to learn new skills from her current volunteer job so that if her former career does not work out, she will have a "back up plan." For Debbie, as a deaf woman, it is perhaps even more critical for her to strategize about different work options. She does this in order to prove to her hearing colleagues, who she describes as "cruel" in terms of making accommodations for her deafness, that she is indeed a valuable worker.

Debbie also actively resists the stigma of being a deaf woman worker, who might be seen by some as unintelligent, by continually challenging herself to improve her English writing skills. This work ethic of "working harder" than hearing women echoes many of the women's educational experiences as they described in chapter three where, in oral schools, they would stay up late to finish their studies. This strategy of working harder comes at a cost to these women since it takes away from having more social time with hearing colleagues as well as places an unfair burden on these deaf women to conform to hegemonic ways of communicating. By conforming to ways of writing and speaking in English, these deaf women, in order to ensure success in hearing workplaces, are faced with political decisions about whether to deny a part of their identity as Deaf women who see ASL as their primary language.

Working in a Predominantly Deaf Environment

Eight of the ten women had, at one time, worked for pay in a predominantly Deaf environment or one where there was a mix of deaf and hearing employees. Five of the ten women currently work in such environments. The five women who do not currently work in such an environment include Teresa who is retired, but who did work in such an environment throughout her professional career, Heather who works in the hearing world, Ellen who currently teaches ASL to hearing families part-time, Debbie who has worked for pay in the hearing world, and Marie who volunteers part-time for her father-in-law's business. All five of the Rochester women and three of the Boston women had then, at one time, worked in a predominately deaf environment. Although the experiences varied, the eight women who had these kinds of jobs said that they felt socially connected in their working environments and that, due to structural things that were in place, such as an office of interpreters or colleagues being part of or familiar with the Deaf community and knowing ASL, their jobs were enjoyable.

Still "Going Back and Forth"

Despite being in predominantly deaf working environments, the women still negotiated going back and forth between worlds. Marie describes an experience of being a Resident Advisor at NTID and how this affected her thinking about being between worlds and going back and forth:

> M: At NTID they have a dormitory with all deaf. And then they have four other hearing. Anybody can go there really. And I wanted to be the Resident Advisor of that deaf dormitory. But, they put me in a hearing dormitory on a special floor interact with deaf and hearing. Each building has one floor of deaf and hearing interacting. So, I was kind of disappointed that I was not part of the deaf building. But, it gave me the opportunity to (She makes a sign that looks like "interact."). And still I struggled interacting with the hearing. They were nice, but it's not the same as deaf. Communicating. My education is in the hearing level. My social is in the deaf level. I can't decide where to go anymore. (She moves her hands back and forth as if in between two groups.) I go back and forth, but I had a good experience.

In this predominantly deaf working environment, part of Marie's work as a deaf woman still involved going back and forth between the worlds, languages, and cultures of the Deaf community and the hearing world. Intellectually, she resonates with the larger hearing society; however, socially she feels more at home with the Deaf community. Even in a predominantly Deaf environment, the women negotiated what it meant to be deaf women. Part of this work involved going back and forth even while working in a predominately Deaf environment. Even when making the political decision to work in a Deaf environment, the women still had to do the identity work of a deaf woman and integrate themselves into the hearing and Deaf worlds.

Carol, after working in the hearing world where she felt somewhat socially isolated, sought a job at an oral state residential school for the deaf:

> Carol: My boss is hard to understand because he's from Iraq. They wanted a deaf person there too. Because there are a lot of deaf staff. So, they said it would be nice to have me to help (She makes a sign that looks like "get together with everyone."). I love my job. There communication is really good. Comfortable. My boss is hearing. And they finally hired another woman who's working for me. She's hearing. But, we have a lot of secretaries, other people who are deaf. I'm the only one deaf in administration. But they all know sign. But, my boss doesn't use sign. I can talk well, so I can use total communication with him. They have an interpreter department there, so if I have a problem, I can make an appointment for me and the interpreter will come. I can go to meetings. Recently, we have a new payroll system. So, I needed to be trained, so I got two interpreters with me. Easy.

As Carol describes, since most of the people in her office know sign, it is easier for her than it was in her all hearing office environment to carry out her day to day responsibilities. Despite the challenge of her boss not knowing sign and being hard to lip read since he is from Iraq, they use a variety of communication methods. Also, at any point in time, Carol can ask for an interpreter to aid in communications with him. Since these structural things are in place in her working environment, she is more easily able to acquire new skills, such as learning the new payroll system, to increase her value as an employee and move up in her career. As with Marie and the other women who worked in predominantly deaf environments, that these women were still doing the work of going back and forth between worlds. A work environment that was predominantly deaf, however, allowed these college educated deaf women to identify more with their Deaf identities than all hearing work environments as they used ASL with colleagues in day to day interactions to develop social connections.

Locations Matter

As mentioned earlier, all five of the Rochester women and three of the Boston women had, at one time, worked in a predominately Deaf environment, which suggests that location or one's community played some role in how these women saw themselves as deaf working women. Rochester women were more likely to have worked in the deaf world and when compared with the Boston women seemed to have a stronger sense of a Deaf community. We see this in the stories of Beth, Janice, and Stephanie who all had spent time at Gallaudet University where they developed strong Deaf identities in their college years. Teresa, who worked as the first deaf secretary in her all hearing department at NTID, describes her experience:

> T: Michael saw an ad that they were looking for a part-time temporary research assistant. Must know how to type. I'm an expert typist. Michael said "typing skills." So, we went over to see someone there and got the job. I was finished with my work, but my contract was still there, so I had to come in. One of the teachers saw me and said, "Will you type up this exam for me?" "Finished? Will, you type something else?" So, she gave me something else. "Finished?" So, she told another teacher. "Can you do this?" It blew their mind, because the other secretary was on the phone, she just couldn't finish her work. So, they asked me "that position why don't you apply for?" "I can't. I'm deaf. I can't use the phone." So, she went to go talk to the chairperson. "We need her." So, they hired me with some modifications. The other secretary would take care of all the phone calls. I would take care of everything else. Because of my typing skills because of the TTYs. So, I could thank the TTY. After eight years, I told my boss I was tired of it. So, he gave me a course to teach. It was Life Skills. So, I would work. Then go teach. But, I only taught part-time. I didn't have a full-time job. But, that was o.k. with me because my number one priority was my family.

Teresa describes how, in part, because of her typing skills she was able to get this job. As she implies, her "disability" actually put her at an advantage, in some ways, to develop the necessary typing skills for this position. As with Beth, in an earlier story in this chapter, Teresa got connected to this job opportunity through her deaf husband who worked as a professor at NTID. They then *together* went to investigate the opportunity in the office. Teresa's personal relationship with her deaf husband, then, played an important role in her career path and opportunities. Location and the larger Deaf community of Rochester also mattered in her obtaining, keeping, and moving up in this job, which led to her, as with Beth, being asked to teach at NTID. Since there were connections between NTID and the Rochester Deaf community, the Rochester women were better able to integrate themselves into this paid deaf work environment at NTID. An all hearing office as part of a larger college for the deaf and Deaf community was one place where these deaf women could find work opportunities. The work opportunities, as described earlier, were often, however, in teaching professions. Another thing that this story, along with Beth's, illustrates is that another strategy that these women used to get jobs was to use their personal connections with their deaf husbands who held jobs in the deaf world.

Another instance where location or community seemingly mattered was in Stephanie's experience of working as a Coordinator in an administrative office at Gallaudet University in another Deaf community:

> S: I had to learn about disabilities. Although, myself I am deaf, it's different because those deaf students with a second disability are challenged. I enjoyed learning about it. Half of them are deaf blind. My office worked, offer services to the group of students. Deaf were fine. Didn't need help. Only deaf with second disability were in the group. Different culture.

Living and working in the D.C. area at Gallaudet where there is a strong Deaf community, being deaf, for Stephanie, was not necessarily seen as a disadvantage. Her office instead assisted those who were deaf and who had another "disability" and thus were culturally different from members of the Deaf community. Differences, then, also existed *within* predominantly deaf working environments. Stephanie, as part of her role in this office and working with this community, was negotiating what it meant to be a deaf woman within as well as between worlds. To do this, part of the work was to consider differences in ability as cultural rather than as differences in one's biological makeup. In this way, Stephanie resisted medical definitions of what it meant to be deaf and viewed deafness as "normal."

BALANCING MOTHERING, PAID WORK, AND ACTIVISM

Like many mothers, the women in this study also had stories of balancing their paid work experiences along with their families. All of the women in this study had worked for pay at some point in their lives and all except for Teresa, who is retired, Debbie, who volunteers for a company and is looking for part-time work, and Marie, who volunteers part-time for her father-in-law's business, are currently employed in either full-time or part-time paid positions. Among the seven women who currently work in paid positions, all but one have full-time jobs, while Ellen works part-time teaching ASL at night. Among the women who currently work for pay, almost all have jobs in the deaf world, except for Heather who works with all hearing people. Debbie works in a hearing office and also in the deaf world with a deaf advocacy group. Marie, who worked in the hearing world in the past, currently still works in the hearing world, however, she does her work out of her home. The influence of these working environments on the women's sense of themselves as mothers as well as on their families also has implications for how they saw themselves as college educated deaf women and how they developed strategies to do this work.

Various researchers have shown how work environments, because they also function as places where people make social connections, relate to how women experience unpaid work (Hochschild, 1997). For the deaf women of this study, this became especially salient in how they conceptualized work and family, as well as what it means to be deaf, hearing, or somewhere in between. The women in this study spoke of wanting to work for pay, the need for flexibility in their working environments along with offices that might make accommodations for their deafness, and the importance of doing activist work with members of the Deaf community. How the women communicated at home and in their workplaces influenced how they thought of themselves as deaf women and how they developed strategies to integrate themselves into these communities. Often, working in a hearing office environment was an opportunity these women used to educate hearing colleagues and their hearing families about the Deaf community.

Paid Work and the Identities of Deaf Women

When the women in this study had children, similar to most women, working for pay became more complicated; however, many were able to negotiate with their bosses or families plans for working at home while remaining at their paid jobs. Seven of the ten women quit their paid jobs at various points to stay-at-home and raise their children. The other three women, Beth who is separated from her husband, Heather who is divorced, and Carol whose husband was laid off, spoke of continuing to work for pay because it was economically necessary.

Professional Working Women are in Our Family

Debbie described how and why she had to convince her husband, Kevin, that she wanted to remain in the paid workforce after she had their two children, despite its not being economically necessary:

D: My mother didn't really stay-at-home. My sister is a doctor herself. My brother's wife is in school now at Harvard. She will work. Her mother worked. Kevin's mother stayed at home. So, there was some clever challenges. "I need to go out. I need to work. I need to (She points to her brain, implying that she needs to think.)." I had to convince my husband, that's what I need to do. And I have my mother explain it to him. You know, I'm not gonna become like your mother, stay-at-home. I'm for people who stay-at-home. I think it's good. Nothing wrong with it. But for me, that's not how I grew up. My mother was always out. My mother did volunteer work, she was a teacher for the deaf, she was (She makes a sign that looks like "doing many things."). So, my husband's getting used to that I am a working mother. I need the support because when the kids are older now, I share more. I talk about work, what I do, what I've learned, I share with them.

By describing how professional working women are in her family history, Debbie also shows that she will pass this ideology on to her two children. Of the seven women who quit their paid jobs to stay-at-home with their children, while five of their own mothers worked for pay and two did not, Debbie was the only one whose mother was college educated and worked as a professional in her field. A key factor, then, in this case, which played a role in whether Debbie would work for pay throughout her child-rearing years was that her own mother also went to college and worked in the paid workforce.

The Importance of Deaf Women Role Models

Debbie continued to explain how working for pay is a particular challenge to deaf women such as herself because, despite her having professional working hearing women in her family as examples of success, she lacked a role model who was a working mother as well as deaf:

D: There are not many deaf mothers, working mothers. Older ones. We're the generation. (She makes a sign that looks like "moving forward.") A lot of deaf mothers stayed at home, but then they found work after the kids have grown and left the house. So, I don't really have a role model in that. So, it makes it even harder. I've always wanted to have a mentor. I think it's important for deaf working mothers to have a mentor. We don't have anybody more experienced than we are. That's what we need. And that's the gap. Because more deaf people are more educated, so they have more power, but they don't have the social structure laid out for them. So, they have to fight for themselves on their own.

So, I use different people for different reasons. I have a list of [people who] I know who I can ask for help. I have different persons for this. I don't have one person. It'd be nice to have that all in one person. I get jealous about some African American people who have their mentor there. They have examples there. They have programs too. And I'm like they say diversity programs, but am I diverse or am I not? I mean [I might ask the question] "do identify myself as disabled, I'm not diverse?" But there's not much for disabled. I think society's perception, how they view "oh disabled people, they can work in a factory. They can work." For some people, it's not true. So, it's hard.

Debbie's comments about professional working women in her family show that the family has a profound influence on a deaf woman's career decisions and opportunities. Despite the cultural capital of having professional working women in her family as role models and her seemingly privileged educational background as college educated, Debbie did not know of any older deaf women who had balanced being a mother with their career. None of the women in this study mentioned having a college educated deaf working mother as a role model or mentor, which suggests that the women in this study are breaking new ground in their roles as college educated deaf mothers and workers. This becomes a crucial piece in understanding the work of these deaf women because it shows that the lack of role models and mentors are critical components to these deaf women's career experiences and opportunities. By working in an all hearing office, Debbie resisted being stereotyped by a larger hearing society as someone "unable" to work.

Debbie, as with all of these women, considers herself as disabled and also a linguistic minority who is part of the Deaf community. The label of being deaf, however, is often not considered similar to other racial and ethnic minorities in the hiring policies and procedures of work places. Instead, the Americans with Disabilities Act (ADA) of 1990 places the deaf under the umbrella term of people with a "disability." As Debbie suggests, until members of the Deaf community are seen in this light by the laws which govern hearing working environments, the advancement of deaf women in the paid workforce will be somewhat limited. Seeking multiple mentors to meet her needs is a strategy which she uses to negotiate her position as a working deaf mother.

Flexibility and Accommodations

Various researchers have looked at the benefits and drawbacks of "flexible" workplaces and the influence they have on women (Martin, 1994;

Hochschild, 1997). There remains little research on how the ideology of flexibility affects women with "disabilities" or those who are deaf. All of the women in this study spoke of wanting to put family first and so, as with many hearing women, flexible working environments where they could vary their schedules were seen as desirable places to work. Additionally, all of them needed to find a workplace environment which was amenable to making accommodations for their deafness. Since accommodations were something they had to advocate for in hearing office settings and not something already in place as in most primarily deaf office environments, this became especially important for the three women, Heather, Debbie, and Marie, who worked for part of their careers in hearing workplaces while also raising their children.

Working "Part Time"

Seven of the women in this study spoke of working part-time so that they might more easily balance their work as mothers with their careers. Definitions of "part time" varied, although all of the women spoke of how working in an office environment where they could communicate more easily with hearing supervisors and colleagues impacted how they negotiated doing part-time work. Marie describes how, at her previous job in a hearing office, she worked part time by working three days a week for ten hours each day:

> M: I LOVED my job there. They were great people. That's why I couldn't leave. I couldn't leave the company. It was just a wonderful company I worked for. They gave me an interpreter. They gave me a TTY (telephone for the deaf). They gave me whatever I asked for. So, I don't want to leave. Better than [my previous company]. I notice that as I get older, my life gets a little bit better with hearing people. I have a little bit more of self esteem. I made friends with a lot of people at that job. I leave the job to take care of the kids. The first two kids I was working part time. But three days a week, ten hours per day. I felt it was easier for me to work ten hours, so I could have my concentration on my work. If I stop at seven hours and go back, I forget where I left off. So, an extra three hours helped speed up my work. My mother-in-law baby sit three days a week. My husband worked nearby. He could pick up. So, he was around to help me out. Pick up the kids. They will work around if I have to. They'd do anything to keep me there.

Marie's story suggests that this office, while making accommodations for her deafness, such as the TTY and interpreter, was an environment where she was also able to negotiate a flexible schedule and work part-time so that she might be at home with her children two days a week. Her story illustrates how she befriended many hearing people at this job, which helped her to negotiate this flexible schedule. Marie told me that she later quit this job after having her fourth child because she wanted to stay-at-home with her children. Like Debbie, who volunteers at a consulting company, Marie also volunteers at her father-in-law's business where she manages his books and tax information. In this way, these two women were able to keep their identity as professional working women. However, their unpaid status shows that this kind of decision along with the ideology of flexibility contributes to the overall disparity of pay for men and women.

Debbie also, similar to Marie, spoke of what it meant to work "part time:"

> D: I'll be working part time for the next ten years. When they're out of the house, I'll go back full-time. Part time means thirty hours a week. (She makes a sign for "quotes" with her hands.) People work forty hours a week or fifty hours a week. Part time is maybe twenty to thirty. It depends on the company. I don't know how to say, this is a full-time job, but I want part time. I cannot say, "oh, I'm a mother. I want part time." I don't like leading them on. That's why I try to time how I'm going to tell them. I had an interview with this company. They liked me, but they don't have the money. This past Thursday I emailed them and I said, "hey look, I'm a mother of two kids. If I was offered a position in mid-April, it would be too late for me to set them up for camp for the summer." Now, I have to be (She makes a sign that looks like "tactful."). There are people who work full-time with two kids. But, I want part time. There's not much conversation about how to handle that kind of situation. A lot of mothers, they just quit completely to take care of the kids. A lot of part time women do retail or homecare. But I'm more into technology. Business. They're also male dominated. I like to be with people. I like to be with data. Some people like to do research. They can do things on their own. It works very well for deaf people. There's no outside communication. I like to be in an interactive mode. If I was not a mother, I would be working full-time all along.

Debbie's comments on how to get a part time job when applying for a full-time position as well as juggling this with her career interests illustrate the differences *within* the experiences of deaf working mothers. For example, as Debbie illustrates, many deaf women are tracked into jobs where little communication is required, such as data management. Because of Debbie's field and training in business, however, these are not suitable working environments for her career and professional development. As mentioned earlier, of all of the women in this study, Debbie, who comes from a strong oral background and family and is married to a hearing man, was the "easiest" person for me to understand. This shows that her skill of spoken English is one which allows her to function in a predominately hearing workplace in a field which relies on oral communication. Debbie's example suggests that gender, ability, and ethnicity, especially when thinking of language as an aspect of ethnicity or ASL as an aspect of what it means to be Deaf, all play a role in the working environments and opportunities for these deaf women.

Working from Home

Two of the deaf women in this study, Heather and Marie, currently work, in part, out of their homes where they do not interact with their hearing colleagues. Heather, who works as a Statistics Analyst and Programmer, has a flexible schedule where she sometimes works from home in order to be with her children:

> H: I get that data and analyze it in a program. I give to my boss. My boss writes reports for journals. Based on the numbers I gave him. My name's in the journals. Not in the top with him, my boss. But, acknowledgments. I have many. I've been with the same job for seven years.

> C: And it sounds like you really enjoy it.

> H: Oh yeah. It's hard to believe, I'm at this job. Similar to what I thought about in high school. I thought about becoming a dietician. RIT has a program. But after looking at the program for career, what they do, not what I want. Like working in the hospital, preparing the food. I tried to avoid a job that required a lot of communication. Involved. Meetings. And this job is perfect for me 'cause I am on the computer all day. I can go to meetings, but there's no interpreter. Because my boss says it's not necessary and there's minutes from the meetings. The secretary would type it up and send out an email. I would read. It's not necessary for me to participate.

> C: So you don't need to have interpreters for the meetings.

> H: I never go to the meetings. I don't see my boss. He's in another building. We send emails back and forth. I like that. 'Cause it's better than pttt (She makes a motion with her hand going over her head like "talking fast."). He emails me a lot of things to do. I can look again.

C: And so the people that you work with, are you social?

H: No. All programmers. And they have different boss. They're doing research too. It's different. Health, some pregnant women. Others diabetes, others different kinds of cancer.

Heather is in a working environment, such as Debbie described, where many deaf women end up since there is little oral communication involved. For Heather, however, she sees her career decision to take a job that requires little personal communication as an effective strategy for working in a hearing society. She enjoys her work and not having to go to meetings so that, as she suggests, she will not feel left out or unable to understand the conversation. Although her career choice is a strategy and effective means of resistance to feeling left out in a hearing workplace that would not make accommodations for her deafness, Heather's example along with Debbie's comments, show that the opportunities of deaf women are sometimes limited to jobs that require little oral communication. Since Heather is divorced and the primary caretaker of her two children, having a flexible workplace so that she might also care for her children takes priority over one that would make accommodations for her deafness. Although she might consider herself a linguistic minority and part of the Deaf community, her employer might not recognize this or consider her "disabled" and thus not supply her with the necessary services for her in the workplace.

CONCLUSION

This chapter has highlighted some of the connections between these deaf women's paid work experiences and opportunities and how they balanced their mothering, paid work, and activism. As the women negotiated what it meant to be deaf women, they made political decisions about being in the Deaf world, hearing world, or somewhere in between often based on how they would communicate in these settings. As seen in chapter four, the ways in which they communicated in their personal relationships and in their current families also influenced some of their decisions to work in a deaf, hearing, or mixed environment.

As seen in Chapter Three, one finding of this study was that the women often made political decisions about their personal relationships in their choices of husbands and friends. That is, they often chose partners and friends who were also Deaf and whose native language was ASL. This was seen as a political decision because they, through these relationships, worked and socialized primarily with members of the Deaf community. As stated in Chapter Three, their experiences of going back and forth between worlds or cultures connects with literature written by women of color who describe their experiences as a kind of border crossing (Ahmed, 2000; Anzaldua, 1990; Lugones, 1990). Although these deaf women had similar experiences, they differ from this body of literature in that they did not literally cross borders into other worlds or countries. Instead, the women in this study experience a kind of border crossing where the boundaries are less tangible. Social relationships were places, then, where the women developed strategies to integrate themselves into hearing and Deaf communities and worlds, which influenced where they worked for pay.

Despite having laws such as the ADA in place, this study has also shown how these deaf women still struggled to overcome obstacles in all hearing offices where their employers would not make accommodations for their deafness. Although some employers did make accommodations, another finding of this study is that, for these women to "succeed" in their work environments, they also needed to have meaningful social relationships with their colleagues and had to work to dispel stereotypes of what it meant for them to be deaf. This echoes scholars who have shown that women of minority races and social classes experience paid work in different ways (Amott & Matthaei, 1996; Sokoloff, 1992). In order to negotiate these differences, the women developed five major strategies to work in all hearing environments including educating their hearing colleagues about deafness, working around hearing employers who would not make accommodations for their deafness, involving hearing family members in their self-advocacy, denying part of their Deaf identity, and volunteering in hearing offices to prove themselves as valuable employees. Especially in all hearing workplaces, deaf women will not have equal access and opportunities in their paid workplaces unless accommodations are made for their deafness and that these work environments strive to dispel stigmas about what it means to be a deaf working woman.

Another finding was that even when working in a predominantly deaf environment, the women still had to go back and forth between worlds in these settings and make political decisions about their identities. For example, these women, who are part of the first generation of college educated deaf women to work in professional positions, often took positions as teachers at schools for the deaf so that they might be seen by a larger hearing society as "legitimate" teachers and workers. In this way, their experiences are similar to scholars who have found that women of minority races are often tracked into particular professions (DeVault, 1999; Sokoloff, 1992). The deaf women in this study were tracked into becoming teachers of the deaf, but also, in part, chose these work settings as places where they might feel at home as well as make a difference in the lives of other deaf people.

This study also found that there were differences *within* these predominantly Deaf working environments. The women developed strategies to integrate themselves into these environments by asking for interpreters and sometimes having their Deaf husbands help them find jobs. One difference in these environments from all hearing offices was that in offices where the staff was predominantly Deaf, there were services in place, such as offices of sign language interpreters as well as an overall climate where most of their hearing colleagues were at the very least familiar with the Deaf community and Deaf culture. These kinds of environments served to help hearing and deaf colleagues communicate with greater ease. As this study found, however, these work environments often existed in particular career sectors and communities, such as teaching in schools for the deaf in places such as Rochester and D.C. These findings illustrate that, despite the experience of being educated orally, the paid work opportunities for these college educated deaf women, especially in the hearing world, are indeed limited.

How the women balanced their mothering, paid work, and activism was another place where they negotiated their identities and made political decisions about themselves. Their experiences of mothering and paid work overlapped as they struggled to find hearing offices where they could have flexibility as well as accommodations made for their deafness. Since this was often difficult to find in such an office environment, many of the women ended up working in deaf offices so that they might better balance their positions as mothers and activists with their paid work experiences.

Chapter Six
Conclusion: The Language Work of Deaf Women

This study examined the work of deaf mothers in their family, educational, and paid work experiences. As my data illustrate, language is key to understandings of both visible and invisible work in family and paid work settings. Although one might think that being bilingual and speaking American Sign Language (ASL) as well as spoken English are an advantage to being "between worlds," the stories of these women show how speaking these two languages sometimes puts them at a disadvantage. As the women try to integrate themselves into various settings, they do a kind of language work where they shift their ways of talking, among using ASL, spoken English, and hybrid languages "in between." As my data show, while making these shifts, they are making political decisions about how they identify themselves. I have shown how this language work is organized and embedded within the larger social contexts of family, education, and the paid workforce. The women do this language work in their family, education, and work settings, in part, to be seen as "good" mothers and workers. By making this work visible, we can see how the work is also maintained by the larger social institutions of work, family, and schools. Since these social institutions and the majority of the people within them use spoken English as the dominant language, those that deviate from this norm, such as the women of this study, are often not seen as legitimate workers, mothers, or women. The women and their families, then, also do this language work, in part, to resist the stigmas often placed on them in hearing and sometimes even in deaf contexts.

Chapter One provided an overview of the major schools of thought related to this project on deaf women and work. This included a discussion of sociologist, feminist, and disability studies scholars' discussions of women's paid and unpaid work, disability and women's work, definitions of disability and deafness, and the "border crossings" and experiences of bilingual women of color. A major goal of this study is to make visible a group of women who have not been adequately represented in these literatures or included in most feminist discussions of women's lives. By looking at the connections between and among these literatures, we can see how by using deaf women as an example, we are able to think about cultural definitions of women, disability, work, and family.

Chapter Two included a discussion of both qualitative and feminist methodologies and how, by using these methods, I was able to look at how these deaf women experience their daily work and family lives. By situating myself in the research process as someone who has a brother who is Deaf and knows Sign Exact English, I argued that I had a certain "insider" status and yet was not part of the Deaf community. This positioning posed interesting methodological challenges and ethical questions involving issues of translation as well as confidentiality. My aim in this chapter was to show how being reflexive, a tenet of feminist methodologies, allowed me to think more closely about this project and the stories of these women's lives as a shared collaboration between myself and the deaf women of this study.

In Chapter Three, I presented an overview and analysis of the deaf women's family, educational experiences, and personal relationships. In this first of three data chapters, I showed how, beginning in their early family experiences, the women often struggled to be included. As they encountered social institutions such as the medical community and schools, the women continued this struggle and developed strategies, they would use throughout their lives, such as lifetime educating and self advocating for their own rights as deaf women. As their family members responded to their deafness, they too worked to integrate the women into various environments in the hearing world.

The women's stories of their motherwork and activism comprised Chapter Four where I analyzed how they made political decisions about communicating with their children and with how they decided to educate their children. For many of these women, activism was a major part of their mothering experiences where they continued to self advocate and educate others about deafness. The women, in particular those who had deaf children, passed these skills on to their children in the hopes of integrating them into schools and the community in both the hearing and Deaf worlds.

Chapter Five consisted of the women's stories of being "between worlds" in their paid work experiences and how they balanced these experiences with their mothering and activism. The data show that many of the women chose and were also tracked into careers in deaf education. Many of the women struggled, in all hearing offices, to become integrated into their office environments and also to have accommodations met for their deafness. Some of the women developed strategies to remain in these hearing offices and work their way up the corporate ladder while others decided to work in the deaf world where communication was easier and there was a shared understanding of the Deaf community. As the women straddled both worlds, they struggled to shift their languages and identities in various settings in order to more easily be integrated into their paid work environments.

SIGNIFICANCE OF THIS STUDY

By gaining insight into the lives of deaf women, I have made visible a population of women who have not been studied at great length. My work explores the paid and unpaid work lives of college educated deaf women in two northeastern cities. It uncovers the places in their lives in which they encounter barriers and also highlights the places where they are able to resist these barriers. Also, by showing that members of the Deaf community are worthy of our scholarly attention, I hope that my work will lead to a greater inclusion of people with disabilities in social science research. My research also poses interesting methodological questions in terms of looking at the researcher and respondent relationship with regards to language and power. It may contribute to ideas of how to do collaborative life history research, especially with women who have a perceived (dis)ability.

As I will later discuss, my work also has led to recommendations for policy changes in how deaf women are educated and employed and recommendations for other services which might assist those women in balancing their paid work and family lives. My data also have implications for laws that govern hiring procedures for women with disabilities, particularly those who are seen as deaf or hard of hearing. Finally, it is possible that my research will shed light on the role of technology with regards to these women's paid and unpaid work lives and experiences.

RETHINKING IDEAS OF WOMEN'S WORK

The feminist movement of the 1960s and 1970s focused on gaining equal employment opportunities and rights for women. Various scholars have argued, however, that the feminist movement was not inclusive of *all* women and left out minority women of color and lesbian women (Bulkin, et., al., 1984; Collins, 2000; hooks, 2000). Other scholars have also recently called for the inclusion of women with disabilities into the feminist movement, discussions of feminist theory, and of women and work (Thomson, 1997). Finally, scholars who write on feminist methodologies argue for an inclusion of all women in research while also thinking of the various methodological issues and challenges (DeVault, 1999; Sandoval, 2000). By focusing our attention to this group of deaf women, we are able to make visible the experiences of such women whose lives may not be widely known and recognized. Also, their stories provide us with insights into how we might think of what it means to be a woman and the relationship between being bilingual and what some term as "disabled" along with ideas about work.

The deaf women in this study have various stories of what it is like to be "between worlds," or part of the hearing world and the Deaf world, and how they often struggle to be included in their family and work settings. Their language choices often help them to identify themselves. Women of color have written about similar experiences of finding a place for themselves and how this relates to being literally or metaphorically bilingual (Anzaldua, 1990; Lugones, 1990). This study connects with these literatures and the stories of other women who experience their lives in terms of being a part of multiple languages and cultures and how this relates to definitions of work.

The findings of this study help us to rethink how scholars have defined women's work to include the experiences of women with a disability or those women who are part of a linguistic minority. This study has shown how gender operates somewhat differently for these deaf women in paid and unpaid work, as it also does for women of various races and economic situations (Amott & Matthaei, 1996). The concept of disability or difference organizes these women in terms of their place in society in their work and family lives. Through the example of this study we see how language work becomes part of the visible and sometimes invisible work of this group of women and also a skill they teach their children. Language work, then, becomes part of the invisible work of being a mother and worker. Those who refuse to do this work or who are unable to do it are further marginalized in the larger English speaking society.

As DeVault (1991) has argued, feeding a family has come to be seen as a type of gendered activity and part of the invisible work of mothers. Harris (2003) examined friendship work as a similar kind of invisible work, which is done by mothers who have children with disabilities. This study has shown that language work is also part of the work of mothers and therefore perhaps a gendered activity. This work, which involves shifting one's language in different contexts, may seem a natural trait of bilingual women. I argue, instead, that it is developed over time and through the process of repeated daily interactions of women in their family, school, and work environments. Following Smith (1999), and viewing language and discourse as a socially organized activity, we can see how using particular languages, such as ASL and spoken English, becomes consequential for these women in their work and family contexts. By making decisions about how they would communicate in their families and work settings, the women located themselves in the larger society as being deaf, hearing, or somewhere in between. Likewise, the language system of a larger hearing society also shaped their experiences, sense of themselves, and their opportunities.

I have shown the enormous amount of work the women do to educate others about deafness and how they advocate for themselves in their family, educational, and work environments. It seems it is the social context, such as the larger hearing society, that makes this possible. Few people in the hearing world took responsibility of this and the women were often left to do this work on their own. The responsibility of this needs to change so that more hearing people also participate in this work in these and other contexts. In this way, both deaf and hearing people will work together to fight oppression.

EDUCATION AS THE BATTLEGROUND

As Lane (1999) has argued, education is the battleground where people of linguistic minorities win or lose their rights. As bilingual women, the women's stories in this study echo his claim. They also add another piece to our understandings of work and how staff and educators at educational institutions, despite efforts at being inclusive, often limit the experiences of such women. The stories of the women of this study along with my analysis, then, differ from Lane's (1999) analysis of taking a mainstreaming or what is often called an inclusive approach to educational policy versus a segregation approach in an all Deaf environment. As I have shown by my analysis, both of these educational philosophies have served to oppress members of the Deaf community. Although I appreciate Lane's argument and have learned a lot from his work, it seems to me that it is possible to strive for an inclusive educational environment where Deaf and hearing individuals are able to use the language of ASL along with spoken English and have a shared understanding of the Deaf community and hearing world.

What needs to change is to have deaf students be integrated into public and private school systems along with the support and services they need while also being able to use their native language of ASL and identify with being part of the Deaf community. In this kind of environment, hearing and deaf students will learn from each other and both have the benefits of being bilingual in terms of learning and using both ASL and spoken English in their daily lives. What follows is a discussion of some of the implications for educational policy.

Implications for Educational Policy

Baynton (1996), who outlines the oralism versus manualism debates of deaf education programs, argues that neither philosophy has been able to accept deaf people as different and also treat them as equals to hearing people. As my data reflect, while oral schools have usually forbidden sign language and employed deaf women as teachers, they were, for the most part, unsuccessful at providing a way to integrate deaf people into a larger hearing workforce. Although most manual schools used ASL, they too did not work to integrate both hearing and deaf students, which often led deaf graduates of manual schools to seek work in deaf environments. As ideas about mainstreaming became popular among education experts in the 1960s, deaf students, such as many of the women in this study, were placed into public and private hearing schools along with hearing students, but without the support of interpreters or deaf education programs. As the women in this study show, this situation was less than ideal, as it often left them at both an educational and social disadvantage. Therefore, the responsibility of integrating themselves into the larger school community was placed almost entirely on these women and their families. Language work became a survival strategy for most of these women, and they learned how to advocate for themselves and educate others about their needs as bilingual deaf women.

Educational philosophies have undergone a shift from mainstreaming to an inclusive approach towards education where parents and educators ideally work together to create a community environment in schools (Biklen, 1992). Other such examples are college campuses recently accepting ASL classes as fulfilling a "foreign" language requirement in their curriculums. Although these are positive first steps, this study has shown that more work needs to be done to ensure an equal opportunity and access to education for all women. For example, more colleges and universities might establish ASL as fulfilling a foreign language requirement in their schools as well as establish a program in Deaf Studies, which similar to Women's Studies, Disability Studies, and African American Studies programs would carve out a space where students might learn histories that are often left out of other courses.

The way in which secondary teachers as well as professors teach their courses might include a variety of mediums, including the use of films, where students might become more aware of ASL as a visual language and something that is often not part of the written texts of classroom discussions. More needs to be done to advance deaf individuals to teach deaf as well as hearing students. By having people who are deaf visible to others in these positions, students as well as educators might learn more about the deaf and work to dispel certain stigmas, including historical ideas of deaf people as "deaf and dumb." Lastly, people with disabilities and those who are part of a linguistic minority, need to be recognized in secondary and postsecondary statements on diversity. This is one way in which it might be possible to include people of multiple backgrounds in an ever changing workforce.

Inclusion and Integration

As Biklen (1992) has discussed, an inclusive educational philosophy involves people with disabilities being integrated into schools as well as the larger society. Using the women in this study as an example, we have seen how critical both elements are to educational and occupational success. Arguing for "purposeful integration," Biklen states that integration needs to come from the parents, the teachers, and the students (p. 147). Schools, then, become communities instead of battlegrounds for people who do not fit the "norm," and those who seemingly do fit can also benefit from the presence of these students.

Since inclusion and integration, then, are necessary components for creating equal educational opportunities, another recommendation for policy makers of educational practices might be to envision schools as extensions of the larger surrounding community. By drawing on the resources of the community and locale of the school, educators might more easily integrate all students into their learning communities. Also, educational policy makers might consider our cultural notions of intelligence and how this seems based on how "well" one speaks English. A model school that aims for inclusion is an environment where all languages are valued and accepted. By using the strengths of all students and teachers, educational policy makers might create school environments where students and teachers collaboratively learn from each other about issues surrounding language, culture, and disability.

Another suggestion might be for schools to conduct focus groups both in the schools systems and local community to ask members of these communities about their educational needs. Leaders of the group and those who have a say in the design of such school policies should include a diverse group of people, including those who have been labeled as "disabled." In this way, everyone might have a say in shaping the policies that would work toward inclusion and integration.

Finally, school officials could look into make curriculum changes where working in the community as a volunteer could become part of a class on service learning. Teachers, students, and members of the community might work together in this way to integrate discussions in the classroom with "hands on" experiences in the community. This would expose students as well as teachers to members of the community, such as volunteering at a Deaf club or organization, and allow for social networking to develop as well as a greater understanding of the Deaf community as well as other minority groups.

THE PERSONAL IS POLITICAL: FAMILIES AS A SITE FOR MOTHERWORK AND ACTIVISM

This study has also shown how the activist work of these women is an integral part of their mothering experiences. The women worked actively to integrate themselves into larger communities. As other scholars have argued, women with a perceived disability have often fought to be seen as legitimate mothers (Reinelt & Fried, 1998; Thomson, 1997). This study shows that language work is a kind of invisible work done by women to be seen as "good" mothers. It also involves making political decisions about one's identity as deaf, Deaf, hearing, or somewhere in between. Through their motherwork and activism, the women performed a kind of language work where they tried to overcome obstacles surrounding being a mother, bilingual, and deaf. Language work, then, also becomes part of the idea that the personal is political, one of the tenets of the feminist movement.

Traustadottir (1992) has shown how mothers of children with disabilities spend much of their time as activists for their children and often, for others as well. The deaf women of this study are activists themselves and also teach their family members, especially deaf children, how to advocate for themselves in their daily lives. Instead of making activist work an individual venture, one way to integrate these families into a community might be to think of ways that activism can become institutionalized and more a part of everyone's lives, including those who might not consider themselves activists. Deaf and hearing people alike will need to work together to fight for inclusive environments in our communities. One way to do this might to be to organize a Deaf Pride day in communities or as part of other community cultural events so that those who might not be familiar with the Deaf community become more knowledgeable about this group. This should not be seen as a quick fix idea, but rather it could serve as a beginning point for opening up future discussions to also include other minority groups.

LIFETIME EDUCATORS AND SELF-ADVOCATES IN PAID WORK ENVIRONMENTS

Implications for Work Environments and Policies

Women with disabilities face a double discrimination on the basis of gender and their perceived disability and have fought to be seen as legitimate workers in the paid workforce (Blackwell-Stratton, et. al., 1988; Russo & Jansen, 1988; Thomson, 1997). This study has shown how language plays a role in women's paid work opportunities. Women who are seen as disabled and part of a linguistic minority are left with the responsibility of doing the language work to ensure their success in their work settings. As the data have shown, they lack the full support of laws, and often face obstacles to social integration into their paid work environments. What needs to happen for these women to have a more equal chance in the workforce is threefold. First, employers need more education about the needs of women with a perceived disability. Second, structures need to be put in place in office environments which encourage social connections at work. Employers might hold seminars on how to successfully collaborate in a multilingual and diverse workplace. Of great importance would be to have deaf as well as hearing workers be part of the planning and implementation of such dialogues and seminars. Supervisors and others in positions of power, both deaf and hearing alike, need to work together to build an office community which is successful and inclusive. Diversity policies in workplaces might work to include deaf people as part of this policy to foster more equal opportunities. There is also a need for tougher laws that ensure accommodations for deaf people in the workforce, such as having sign language interpreters and note takers in meetings and having a TTY in offices where deaf people work. There also need to be people who are in a position to check that companies are following these laws to make accommodations for deafness. Finally, there needs to be a willingness on the part of the federal government to pay for technological aids, such as a TTY and other devices, which can assist these women and others in their work environments.

Building a Community at Work

As Groce (1985) and Higgins (1980) have shown, the common language of a community and the stigmas attached to people who do not speak it depend on time and place. Thus, if efforts were made to socially integrate women into the workforce, such as those of this study, stigmas about their being seen as unable to do certain jobs have the potential to change.

Stephanie, quoted earlier, said it best when she commented that education or the language work has to come from the hearing people in the office environments as well as the women of this study. Although there will always be language differences and communication struggles between people who do not speak similar languages, building an office community which is inclusive of all women would help dispel certain myths about women whose native language is not spoken English.

Scholars have recently written about how to be inclusive in paid work settings and the need for people with disabilities to have a voice in the creation of workforce policies (Crow & Foley, 2002; Hoff, 2000). By changing some of the existing power dynamics that exist in hearing offices, workers would be more likely to foster a productive as well as inclusive community. As stereotypes are slowly broken down, we might begin to see offices which would represent more of an inclusive environment, which supports the different lives of individual people.

Reaching out to the Community

Another way in which offices might build bridges with members of the Deaf community as well as other minority groups, might be to follow the model of some schools. Perhaps offices might do their part to strengthen their ties with members of their surrounding community. They might organize social events such as job fairs or an "open house" that get various groups together from the community to interact and network. Another possible option would be for offices to hold training seminars and workshops for those interested in working at their company and to eventually hire people from these seminars.

STUDY LIMITATIONS AND FUTURE RESEARCH

There are several areas which could be pursued as future research. First, one limitation of this study was that the majority of the women were white and economically comfortable. Though there was some ethnic and economic diversity among the women studied, it would be beneficial to include women of varying other backgrounds to gain a fuller understanding of women's language work and how it informs ideas of women, mothers, disability, and work. By looking at women of different races and classes, we might be able to understand how race and class work in conjunction with gender and ability. Also, within the Deaf community, the group of women of this study are in many ways the most integrated and visible in a larger hearing society. As this group is made visible to those who might not have known much about them, scholars will need to learn more about the experiences of other deaf women and how these experiences vary *within* the Deaf community. For example, it would be helpful to see how the experiences might be similar or different for women of different educational backgrounds and who do not have the privilege of a college education. Variations in age would also help us to understand more about how the experiences of deaf women may have changed over time. Also, it would be important to look at the experiences of lesbian deaf women who might face additional struggles to be seen, by some, as visible and legitimate mothers.

As Sokoloff (1992) has shown, black women are often tracked into certain professions on the basis of their gender and race. It would be interesting to gather more data to see if college educated deaf women are tracked into other professions in addition to teaching at schools and colleges for the deaf as this study suggests. How might this differ for those women who do not live near a school or college for the deaf or in a Deaf community? How similar or different are the experiences of women in other states or parts of the world?

Another area of future research might be to look at other women who are considered part of a linguistic minority. How might the experiences of non native English speaking women in the workforce who are not seen as disabled compare with this group of women? Are there similar needs in terms of what needs to be done to ensure equality and chances for advancement in the paid workforce?

A third area for future research would be to look at the work of deaf and hard of hearing fathers. Research on fathers has recently become an important part of the literature on families and disability (Berube, 1996; Spradley & Spradley, 1985). Scholars have also begun looking at masculinity and how it relates to having a physical disability (Gerschick & Miller, 1995). There is, however, little research done on fathers who are seen as having a disability and how they experience their work and family lives. These stories might help us to gain a fuller understanding of how definitions of the family as a social institution are upheld by larger cultural ideas about mothers and fathers. It could also investigate whether fathers also do language work and if so, how it might be similar or different from the women in this study.

Another area for future research might be interviewing the children of deaf mothers who are either deaf, hard of hearing, or hearing to see how they experience their work and family lives. Autobiographies of adults who recount their childhood experiences as well as some of the data from this study show that children also perform a kind of language work. Various authors who are children of deaf parents, have another deaf relative, or who are deaf themselves have written about such family experiences

(Cohen, 1994; Herring Wright, 1999; Jacobs, 1989; Kisor, 1990; Spradley & Spradley, 1978; Walker, 1986). Since most of these literatures take the form of personal memoirs, it would be interesting to provide a sociological analysis of such experiences while making various connections with the deaf women of this study and our larger ideas of work, family, and disability.

This study has shown the work and family lives of a group of deaf women and how their experiences as part of a linguistic minority in a larger hearing society are often a story of struggles to be seen, by some, as mothers and workers. Readers of this study who had little prior knowledge of this group of women as well as those with experience or who might be Deaf themselves might think of various questions to take with them in their own work and family lives. How does this story inform our ideas of women, families, work, deafness, and disability? In what ways can our schools, communities, and work environments be inclusive of all people of various languages and cultures? How might we teach our children about such issues and what can they teach us? These questions are critical ones that we need to ask in our efforts to combat issues of racism, sexism, abelism, and other inequalities in our stratified society. It is my hope and belief that, through the efforts of *all* of these groups of people along with educational changes and policies and laws which address issues of inclusion, we will create spaces where all people are treated with respect and dignity. This project invites readers to rise to the challenges and triumphs of creating such a place.

Interview Questions Guide

Interviewee:_____

Date:_____

Time:_____

Location:_____

1) Where did you attend school?

2) What were your school experiences like?

3) Can you tell me about your first job experience?

4) Can you trace your work history for me?

5) What kinds of jobs have you held and what were those experiences like?

6) Please tell me a bit about your family.

7) What do you see as your role in your family?

8) What is the role of your partner? (if applicable)

9) What is the role of each of your children? (if applicable)

10) How do you communicate with each of the members of your family?

11) Is there anything that you would like to add to describe either your educational, work, or family history?

12) Do you know of any other deaf, Deaf, or hard of hearing women in Rochester or Boston who might like to participate?

Name:_____ Email:_____

Name:_____ Email:_____

Mother's Day Letter

May 1, 2003

Dear:

I wanted to take this opportunity to wish all of you a very **HAPPY MOTHER'S DAY**! Thank you again for volunteering your time to be a part of my research study on deaf moms and work. I must say that meeting all of you and hearing your stories has been the highlight of this process for me. Each one of you has shared so much and has been a valuable part of the story that I am trying to tell.

A brief update on the study is that I have completed all of my interviews! Hooray! I've (as you know) interviewed 5 women in Rochester, NY and 5 in Boston, MA. I've been busy all winter typing up the interview dialogues and trying to identify the main themes. I will begin writing my analysis this May.

Sometime in the next week or so, I am going to send out an email asking you some BRIEF questions in terms of follow up. What I thought would be neat would be to get YOUR opinions on reactions to the main themes which I have identified in the stories. This is my attempt at trying to make this project collaborative! :) I'll also ask for some brief demographic information, so that when I begin writing I can easily summarize your stories. Hope this sounds good with you!

Again, it is with heartfelt thanks that I send you this little note wishing some of the most AMAZING MOMS that I have ever met a Mother's Day greeting! I thank you for touching my life with each of your stories and for making a difference in my life and in the lives of others.

If you need to get in touch with me, feel free to email me at my enclosed email address.

Warmest,

Cheryl :)

Appendix C
Follow-up Interview Questions Guide

Interviewee:

Date:

Part 1: *Demographic Information:*

1) What do you consider to be your race or ethnicity?

2) Which of the following best describes your family's economic status?

      a. very comfortable

      b. comfortable

      c. somewhat comfortable

      d. struggling to get along

Answer:

3) What is your religion?

4) How might you identify yourself regarding the terms Deaf, deaf, and hard of hearing and why?

5) Do you have any visible or invisible "disabilities" or health conditions that we did not discuss in our interview?

Part 2: *Follow-up Questions on Main Themes:*

1) When talking of first learning sign language, many of you spoke of it as "picking up a language" and describe "going back and forth" from ASL to Sign Exact English. For some of you, this topic also came up when you described your children's communication styles and language(s). Is there

anything else that you would like to add regarding these themes or any other examples that you would like to share?

2) Many of you described being a "self-advocate" in various situations both in and outside of the paid workforce. Some of you also spoke of teaching your kids to do this. Is there anything else that you would like to add regarding this theme or any other examples that you would like to share?

3) Many of you spoke of being "lifetime educators" both in and outside of the paid workforce. Is there anything else that you would like to add regarding this theme or any other examples that you would like to share?

4) Is there anything else that you would like to add to describe either your educational, work, or family history that we did not get a chance to discuss in our interview?

Part 3: *Clarifying Questions from Our Interview:*

1) Note: This section varied by respondent.

Thank you again so much for your time and thoughts!

Tables

Table 1: Respondent Demographics: Rochester Women

Beth	Stephanie
Age: 41	**Age:** 45
Race: White	**Race:** White
Social Class: Economically Comfortable	**Social Class:** Economically Comfortable
Religion: None	**Religion:** Catholic
Deaf/deaf/hard of hearing: Deaf	**Deaf/deaf/hard of hearing:** Deaf
Education: manual school, public school, Gallaudet, NTID—AAS in Mechanical Art, NTID/RIT—BFA, MS in ASL teaching.	**Education:** public school, manual school, Gallaudet—BA in Communication Arts and Deaf Studies, NTID–graduate work, Secondary Ed.
Marital Status: Separated; hard of hearing husband	**Marital Status:** Married; Deaf husband.
Children: hearing daughter, age 14; hearing son, age 9.	**Children:** hearing Sara, age 16; hearing Maureen, age 14; hearing Robbie, age 11.
Occupation: Assistant Professor at NTID.	**Occupation:** Homemaker, ASL Specialist at school for Deaf, deaf blind interpreter.
Family Growing Up: All hearing family.	**Family Growing Up:** All hearing, older deaf sister.
Language: Native ASL speaker.	**Language:** ASL native speaker.
Other: Interpreter—Hannah; present for interview.	*(continued)*

Table 1: Respondent Demographics: Rochester Women (continued)

Kristen	Teresa
Age: 38	**Age:** 63
Race: White	**Race:** White
Social Class: Economically Comfortable	**Social Class:** Economically Comfortable
Religion: Catholic	**Religion:** Southern Baptist
Deaf/deaf/hard of hearing: Deaf	**Deaf/deaf/hard of hearing:** Deaf
Education: private hearing school, oral school, private hearing elementary—high school, small, all women's hearing college (2 years), NTID/RIT—BA in Social Work, hearing university.—MA in Social Work.	**Education:** oral school, public school, small all women's college—BA in Home Economics, hearing university—MA in Women's Studies.
Marital Status: Married; Deaf husband.	**Marital Status:** Married; Deaf husband.
Children: deaf son, age 10; deaf daughter, age 8.	**Children:** hearing Steve, age 37; hearing Kimberly, age 36; hearing Sandy, age 32.
Occupation: Counselor and teacher at NTID.	**Occupation:** Retired, volunteers for Deaf Women organization. Last job: Secretary at NTID and taught part time, editor of Deaf newsletter.
Family Growing Up: All hearing family.	**Family Growing Up:** All hearing.
Language: Raised as an oralist. ASL speaker. Also uses cued speech.	**Language:** Raised as an oralist. "Not native" ASL speaker, but uses it.
Janice	
Age: 47	
Race: Jewish	
Social Class: Economically Comfortable	
Religion: Jewish	
Deaf/deaf/hard of hearing: Deaf	
Education: oral school, Gallaudet—BA in Social Work and Psychology, Gallaudet—MA in Education for the deaf, hearing university—Certificate in Ed. Admin. (in progress).	
Marital Status: Married; Deaf husband.	
Children: deaf son, age 18; deaf daughter, age 15.	
Occupation: Director at school for Deaf.	
Family Growing Up: All deaf family.	
Language: Raised as an oralist. ASL speaker.	

Table 2: Respondent Demographics: Boston Women

Carol	Debbie
Age: 39	**Age:** 39
Race: White	**Race:** White
Social Class: Economically Comfortable	**Social Class:** Somewhat Economically Comfortable
Religion: Catholic	**Religion:** Catholic
Deaf/deaf/hard of hearing: Deaf	**Deaf/deaf/hard of hearing:** Deaf
Education: oral school, public school, NTID—AAS in Business, went to NTID/RIT for some time.	**Education:** preschool for deaf, public school, oral school, small, private, hearing school, small, religiously affiliated college—BA, Psychology, large university—BSBA, business school—MBA.
Marital Status: Married; Deaf husband	
Children: hearing daughter, age 6.	**Marital Status:** Married; hearing husband.
Occupation: Assistant Controller at school for deaf.	**Children:** hearing son, age 10; hearing daughter, age 6.
Family Growing Up: All hearing.	**Occupation:** Homemaker, volunteers at consulting company, volunteers at a deaf organization.
Language: Raised as an oralist. ASL.	**Family Growing Up:** All hearing.
	Language: Raised as an oralist. ASL, but signs and speaks with English grammatical order.
Heather	**Marie**
Age: 36	**Age:** 38
Race: White	**Race:** White
Social Class: Somewhat Economically Comfortable	**Social Class:** Economically Comfortable
Religion: None, but "believes in Jesus"	**Religion:** Lutheran, but raising kids Catholic
Deaf/deaf/hard of hearing: deaf	**Deaf/deaf/hard of hearing:** Deaf
Education: preschool for deaf, public school, small, hearing college (2 years), NTID/RIT—BA in Biology, NTID/RIT—MA in Statistics.	**Education:** public school, NTID—AAS in Data Processing, RIT—BS in Information Systems.
Marital Status: Divorced; Deaf ex-husband.	**Marital Status:** Married; hard of hearing husband.
Children: hearing Brian, age 9; hearing Jeffrey, age 5. *(continued)*	**Children:** hearing daughter, age 10; hearing son, age 8; hearing son, age 4; hearing son age 18 months. *(continued)*

Table 2: Respondent Demographics: Boston Women (continued)

Heather (continued)	Marie (continued)
Occupation: Statistics Analyst/Programmer at hearing university. **Family Growing Up:** Hearing parents and younger brother, youngest brother is deaf. **Language:** Raised as an oralist. Uses ASL but also signs and speaks in English grammatical order.	**Occupation:** Homemaker, works part-time for father-in-law doing taxes and paperwork, volunteers as her daughter's Girl Scout Troop leader. **Family Growing Up:** All hearing. **Language:** Raised as an oralist. ASL, but signs and speaks with English grammatical order.
Ellen **Age:** 34 **Race:** White **Social Class:** Somewhat Economically Comfortable **Religion:** None **Deaf/deaf/hard of hearing:** Deaf **Education:** oral school, public school, college (3 y). **Marital Status:** Divorced; first husband, deaf; Remarried; second husband Deaf. **Children:** Deaf Kate, age 2; Deaf Elise, age 6 wks. **Occupation:** Homemaker, part-time ASL teacher. **Family Growing Up:** Hearing parents, 3 older hearing brothers, one younger hearing sister, fourth older brother is Deaf. **Language:** Raised an oralist. ASL. **Other:** Husband—Peter; present for our interview.	

Notes

NOTES TO CHAPTER TWO

1. See Tables 1 and 2 for Respondent Demographics.
2. See Appendix A for my Interview Questions Guide.
3. See Appendix B for the Mother's Day letter.
4. See Appendix C for my Follow-Up Interview Questions Guide.
5. All names are pseudonyms.

Bibliography

Ahmed, S. (2000). *Strange Encounters: Embodied Others in Post-Coloniality.* New York: Routledge.

Amott, T. & Matthaei, J. (1996). *Race, Gender, and Work: A Multi-cultural Economic History of Women in the United States* (Rev. ed.). Boston: South End Press.

Anzaldua, G. (1990). Haciendo caras, una entrada: An Introduction. In G. Anzaldua (Ed.), *Making Face, Making Soul, Haciendo Caras: Creative Critical Perspectives by Feminists of Color* (pp. xv-xxviii). San Francisco: Aunt Lute Books.

Anzaldua, G. (1990). La conciencia de la mestiza: Towards a new Consciousness. In G. Anzaldua (Ed.), *Making Face, Making Soul, Haciendo Caras: Creative Critical Perspectives by Feminists of Color* (pp. 377–389). San Francisco: Aunt Lute Books.

Asch, A. & Fine, M. (1997). Nurturance, Sexuality and Women With Disabilities: The Example of Women and Literature. In L. J. Davis (Ed.), *The Disability Studies Reader* (pp. 241–259). New York: Routledge.

Barnartt, S. N. (1997). Gender Differences in Changes Over Time: Educations and Occupations of Adults With Hearing Losses, 1972–1991. *Journal of Disability Policy Studies, 8,* No. 1, 2, 7–24.

Bauman, L. H. Dirksen & Drake, J. (1997). Silence Is Not Without Voice: Including Deaf Culture within Multicultural Curricula. In L. J. Davis (Ed.), *The Disability Studies Reader* (pp. 307–311). New York: Routledge.

Baynton, D. C. (1996). *Forbidden Signs: American Culture and the Campaign Against Sign Language.* Chicago: The University of Chicago Press.

———. (1997). "A Silent Exile on This Earth:" The Metaphorical Construction of Deafness in the Nineteenth Century. In L. J. Davis (Ed.), *The Disability Studies Reader* (pp. 128–150). New York: Routledge.

Becker, H. S. (1963). *Outsiders: Studies in the Sociology of Deviance.* New York: Free Press.

Berger, P. L., & Luckmann, T. (1966). *The Social Construction of Reality: A Treatise in the Sociology of Knowledge.* New York: Anchor Books.

Berube, M. (1996). *Life as We Know It: A Father, a Family, and an Exceptional Child*. New York: Vintage Books.

Best, A. (2003). Doing Race in the Context of Feminist Interviewing: Constructing Whiteness Through Talk. *Qualitative Inquiry, 10, No. 10*, 1–20.

Biklen, D. (1992). *Schooling without Labels: Parents, Educators, and Inclusive Education*. Philadelphia: Temple University Press.

Blackwell-Stratton, M., et. al. (1988). Smashing Icons: Disabled Women and the Disability and Women's Movements. In M. Fine & Asch, A. (Eds.), *Women with Disabilities: Essays in Psychology, Culture, and Politics* (pp. 306–332). Philadelphia: Temple University Press.

Bogdan, R. (1988). *Freak Show: Presenting Human Oddities for Amusement and Profit*. Chicago: The University of Chicago Press.

Bogdan, R. & Biklen, D. (1977). Handicapism. *Social Policy, March/April*, 14—19.

Bogdan, R. C., & Biklen, S. K. (1998). *Qualitative Research for Education: An Introduction to Theory and Methods*. Boston: Allyn and Bacon.

Bogdan, R. & Taylor, S. (1987). Toward a sociology of acceptance: The other side of the study of deviance. *Social Policy, 18*, 34–39.

———. (1994). *The Social Meaning of Mental Retardation: Two Life Stories*. New York: Teachers College Press.

Brueggemann, B. J. (1999). *Lend Me Your Ear: Rhetorical Constructions of Deafness*. Washington, D.C.: Gallaudet University Press.

Bruyere, S. M. (Ed.), (2004). *Implementing the Americans with Disabilities Act: Working Effectively with Persons who are Deaf or Hard of Hearing*. University of Arkansas Research and Training Center for Persons who are Deaf or Hard of Hearing. [On-line]. Available: http://www.uark.edu/depts/rehabres/cornell.html.

Bulkin, E., et., al. (1984). *Yours in Struggle: Three Feminist Perspectives on Anti-Semitism and Racism*. Ithaca: Firebrand Books.

Buriel, R., et. al. (1998). The Relationship of Language Brokering to Academic Performance, Biculturalism, and Self-Efficacy among Latino Adolescents. *Hispanic Journal of Behavioral Sciences, August*, 283–297.

Cohen, L. H. (1994). *Train Go Sorry: Inside a Deaf World*. New York: Vintage Books.

Collins, P. H. (2000). *Black Feminist Thought: Knowledge, Consciousness, and the Politics of Empowerment* (2nd ed.). New York: Routledge.

Coltrane, S. (2000). *Gender and Families*. New York: Rowman and Littlefield Publishers, Inc.

Crow, K. & Foley, S. (2002). A Common Path: Navigating your Way to Successful Negotiations in the Workplace. *Institute for Community Inclusion, September*, 1–7. [On–Line]. Available: http://www.communityinclusion.org/publications/pub.php?page=women2.

Daniels, A. K. (1987). Invisible Work. *Social Problems, 34*, 403–415.

Davis, L. J. (1997). Universalizing Marginality: How Europe Became Deaf in the Eighteenth Century. In L. J. Davis (Ed.), *The Disability Studies Reader* (pp. 110–127). New York: Routledge.

———(Ed.). (1999). *Shall I Say a Kiss?: The Courtship Letters of a Deaf Couple 1936-1938*. Washington, D.C.: Gallaudet University Press.

De Andrade, L. L. (2000). Negotiating from the Inside: Constructing Racial and Ethnic Identity in Qualitative Research. *Journal of Contemporary Ethnography, 29, No. 3,* 268–290.

de Cristoforo, V. K. (1987). Affidavit of Violet Kazue de Cristoforo: Challenging the inaccurate, misleading and denigrating references and accusations made by Rosalie Hankey Wax in *Doing Fieldwork: Warnings and Advice,* and in *The Spoilage,* at Tule Lake, California, 1944–45, 1–66.

DeVault, M. L. (1991*). Feeding the Family: The Social Organization of Caring as Gendered Work.* Chicago: The University of Chicago Press.

———. (1999). Comfort and Struggle: Emotion Work in Family Life, *The Annals of the American Academy, 661, January,* 53–63.

———. (1999). Ethnicity and Expertise: Racial-Ethnic Knowledge in Sociological Research. In M. L. DeVault, *Liberating Method: Feminism and Social Research* (pp. 84–103). Philadelphia: Temple University Press.

———. (1999). Talking Back to Sociology: Distinctive Contributions of Feminist Methodology. In M. L. DeVault, *Liberating Method: Feminism and Social Research* (pp. 25–45). Philadelphia: Temple University Press.

Emerson, R. M. (Ed.). (2001). *Contemporary Field Research: Perspectives and Formulations* (2nd ed.). Prospect Heights, IL: Waveland Press, Inc.

Foster, S. (2001). Examining the Fit Between Deafness and Disability. In S. N. Barnartt & Altman, B. M. (Eds.), *Exploring Theories and Expanding Methodologies: Where we are and Where we Need to Go.* New York: Elsevier Science Ltd.

Galinsky, E. (2001). Toward a New View of Work and Family Life. In R. Hertz & Marshall, N. L. (Eds.), *Working Families: The Transformation of the American Home* (pp. 168–186). Berkeley: University of California Press.

Gerschick, T. J. & Miller, A S. (1995). Coming to Terms: Masculinity and Physical Disability. In M. S. Kimmel & Messner M. A. (Eds.), *Men's Lives* (3rd ed.) (pp. 262–275). Boston: Allyn and Bacon.

Gerson, K. & Jacobs, J. A. (2001). Changing the Structure and Culture of Work: Work and Family Conflict, Work Flexibility, and Gender Equity in the Modern Workplace. In R. Hertz & Marshall, N. L. (Eds.), *Working Families: The Transformation of the American Home* (pp. 207–226). Berkeley: University of California Press.

Glazer, B. G. & Strauss, A. L. (1967). *Discovery of Grounded Theory: Strategies for Qualitative Research.* Chicago: Aldine.

Glenn, E. N. (1987). Racial ethnic women's labor: The intersection of race, gender, and class oppression. In C. Bose, et, al. (Eds.), *Hidden Aspects of Women's Work.* New York: Praeger.

Goffman, E. (1959). *The Presentation of Self in Everyday Life.* New York: Doubleday.

———. (1963). *Stigma: Notes on the Management of Spoiled Identity.* New Work: Simon and Schuster, Inc.

Griffith, A. I. (1995). Mothering, Schooling, and Children's Development. In M. Campbell & Manicom, A. (Eds.), *Knowledge, Experience, and Ruling Relations: Studies in the Social Organization of Knowledge* (pp. 108–121). Buffalo: University of Toronto Press.

Griffith, A. I. & Smith, D. E. (1987). Constructing Cultural Knowledge: Mothering as Discourse. In J. Gaskell & McLaren, A. (Eds.), *Women and Education: A Canadian Perspective.* (2nd ed.). Calgary: Detselig Enterprises.

Groce, N. (1985). *Everyone Here Spoke Sign Language: Hereditary Deafness on Martha's Vineyard.* Cambridge: Harvard University Press.

Gubrium, J. & Holstein, J. (1990). *What is Family?* Mountain View: Mayfield Publishing, Co.

Harrington Meyer, M. (2000). *Care Work: Gender, Labor, and the Welfare State.* New York: Routledge.

Harris, P. (2003). *"Mom will do it:" The Organization and Implementation of Friendship Work for Children with Disabilities.* Unpublished dissertation, Syracuse University.

Hays, S. (1996). *The Cultural Contradictions of Motherhood.* New Haven: Yale University Press.

Herring Wright, M. (1999). *Sounds Like Home: Growing up Black and Deaf in the South.* Washington, D.C.: Gallaudet University Press.

Hertz, R., & Marshall, N. L. (2001). Introduction. In R. Hertz & Marshall, N.L. (Eds.), *Working Families: The Transformation of the American Home* (pp. 1–20). Berkeley: University of California Press.

———. (2001). *Working Families: The Transformation of the American Home.* Berkeley: University of California Press.

Higgins, P. (1980). *Outsiders in a Hearing World: A Sociology of Deafness.* Beverly Hills: Sage Publications, Inc.

Hochschild, A. R. (1983). *The Managed Heart: Commercialization of Human Feeling.* Berkeley: University of California Press.

———. (1989). *The Second Shift.* New York: Avon Books.

———. (1997). *The Time Bind: When Work Becomes Home and Home Becomes Work.* New York: Henry Holt and Company.

Hoff, D. (2000). People with Disabilities: Having a Voice in the Creation of the New Workforce Investment System. *Tools for Inclusion, 8, No. 2, March,* 1–9. [On-Line]. Available: http://www.communityinclusion.org/publications/text/voice.html.

Holstein, J. A. & Gubrium, J. F. (1995). The Active Interview in Perspective. *Qualitative Research Methods: The Active Interview, 37,* 7–18.

Holt, J., et., al. (2002). *Demographic Aspects of Hearing Impairment: Questions and Answers* (3rd ed., 1994). Gallaudet Research Center. [On-line]. Available: http://gri.gallaudet.edu/demographics/factsheet.html.

hooks, b. (2000). *Feminist Theory: From Margin to Center* (2nd ed.). Cambridge: South End Press.

Jacobs, J. A. (1995). Introduction. In J. A. Jacobs (Ed.), *Gender Inequality at Work* (pp. 1–20). Thousand Oaks: Sage Publications.

Jacobs, L. M. (1989). *A Deaf Adult Speaks Out* (3rd ed.). Washington, D.C.: Gallaudet University Press.

Kisor, H. (1990). *What's that Pig Outdoors?: A Memoir of Deafness.* New York: Penguin Books.

Lane, H. (1997). Constructions of Deafness. In L. J. Davis (Ed.), *The Disability Studies Reader* (pp. 153–171). New York: Routledge.

————. (1999). *The Mask of Benevolence: Disabling the Deaf Community.* San Diego: DawnSign Press.

Linton, S. (1998). *Claiming Disability: Knowledge and Identity.* New York: New York University Press.

Lorber, J. (1994). *Paradoxes of Gender.* New Haven: Yale University Press.

Lugones, M. (1990). Playfulness, "World"-Travelling, and Loving Perception. In G. Anzaldua (Ed.), *Making Face, Making Soul, Haciendo Caras: Creative Critical Perspectives by Feminists of Color* (pp. 390–402). San Francisco: Aunt Lute Books.

Lupton, D. & Barclay, L. (1997). *Constructing Fatherhood: Discourses and Experiences.* Thousand Oaks: Sage Publications.

Martin, E. (1994). *Flexible Bodies: The Role of Immunity in American Culture from the Days of Polio to the Age of Aids.* Boston: Beacon Press.

Maynard, M. (2001). "Race," Gender and the Concept of "Difference" in Feminist Thought. In K. K. Bhavnani (Ed.), *Feminism and Race.* England: Oxford.

Mitchell, R. (2002). *Can you Tell How Many Deaf People there are in the United States?* Gallaudet Research Center. [On-line]. Available: http://gri.gallaudet.edu/demographics/deaf-US.html.

Moen, P. & Han, S. K. (2001). Gendered Careers: A Life-Course Perspective. In R. Hertz & Marshall, N. L. (Eds.), *Working Families: The Transformation of the American Home* (pp. 42–57). Berkeley: University of California Press.

Najarian, C. G. (2002, May). *On the Life History of a Deaf Woman.* Paper presented at the Fieldwork in Contemporary Society Conference, Los Angeles, CA.

Naples, N. A. (1998). *Grassroots Warriors: Activist Mothering, Community Work, and the War on Poverty.* New York: Routledge.

National Association of the Deaf (NAD) website. 2002. [On–Line]. Available: http://www.nad.org/about/index.html.

National Association of the Deaf (NAD) Position Statement on Cochlear Implants. 2000. [On–Line]. Available: http://www.nad.org/infocenter/newsroom/positions/CochlearImplants.html.

Padden, C. & Humphries, T. (1988). *Deaf in America: Voices from a Culture.* Cambridge: Harvard University Press.

Reinelt, C. & Fried, M. (1998). "I am This Child's Mother": A Feminist Perspective on Mothering with a Disability. In K. Hansen & Garey, A. (Eds.), *Families in the US: Kinship and Domestic Politics.* Philadelphia: Temple University Press.

Reinharz, S. (1992). *Feminist Methods in Social Research.* New York: Oxford University Press.

Reskin, B. & Padavic, I. (2002). *Women and Men at Work* (2nd Ed.). Thousand Oaks: Pine Forge Press.

Reskin, B. & Roos, P. (1990). *Job Queues, Gender Queues: Explaining Women's Inroads into Male Occupations.* Philadelphia: Temple University Press.

Russo, N. F. & Jansen, M. A. (1988). Women, Work, and Disability: Opportunities and Challenges. In M. Fine & Asch, A. (Eds.), *Women with Disabilities: Essays in Psychology, Culture, and Politics* (pp. 229–244). Philadelphia: Temple University Press.

Sandoval, C. (2000). *Methodology of the Oppressed.* Minneapolis: University of Minnesota Press.

Shapiro, J. P. (1996). "The Deaf Celebration of Separate Culture." In J. P. Shapiro, *No Pity: People with Disabilities Forging a New Civil Rights Movement* (pp. 74–104). New York: Three Rivers Press.

Shostak, M. (1983). *Nisa: The Life and Words of a !Kung Woman*. New York: Vintage Books.

Smith, R.C. (1996). *A Case About Amy*. Philadelphia: Temple University Press.

Smith, D. E. (1987). *The Everyday World as Problematic: A Feminist Sociology*. Boston: Northeastern University Press.

———. (1999). *Writing the Social: Critique, Theory, and Investigations*. Buffalo: University of Toronto Press.

Sokoloff, N. J. (1992). *Black Women and White Women in the Professions*. New York: Routledge.

Spradley, T. S. & Spradley, J. P. (1978). *Deaf Like Me*. Washington, D.C.: Gallaudet College Press.

Stone, P. (1995). Assessing Gender at Work: Evidence and Issues. In J. A. Jacobs (Ed.), *Gender Inequality at Work* (pp. 408–423). Thousand Oaks: Sage Publications.

Taylor, S. J. (2000). "You're Not a Retard, You're Just Wise:" Disability, Social Identity, and Family Networks. *Journal of Contemporary Ethnography, Vol. 29, No. 1*, 58–92.

Taylor, S. J., & Bogdan, R. (1998). *Introduction to Qualitative Research Methods* (3rd ed.). New York: John Wiley and Sons, Inc.

Thomson, R. G. (1997). *Extraordinary Bodies: Figuring Physical Disability in American Culture and Literature*. New York: Columbia University Press.

———. (1997). Feminist Theory, the Body, and the Disabled Figure. In L. J. Davis (Ed.), *The Disability Studies Reader* (pp. 279–306). New York: Routledge.

Traustadottir, R. (1992). *Disability Reform and the Role of Women: Community Inclusion and Caring Work*. Unpublished dissertation, Syracuse University.

Walker, L. A. (1986). *A Loss for Words: The Story of Deafness in a Family*. New York: Harper and Row, Publishers.

Weedon, C. (1999). *Feminism, Theory, and the Politics of Difference*. Malden: Blackwell Publishers.

Wendell, S. (1996). *The Rejected Body: Feminist Philosophical Reflections on Disability*. New York: Routledge.

Index